Ordinary Shoes on Sacred Ground

There, God Was Also

By

LINDA PERRY & JOY LECHIEN

This is a work of nonfiction. Some names and identifying details may have
been changed to protect privacy, but all stories were submitted with
permission.

For story inquiries, permissions, or to share your own sacred story, please
contact:
sacredgroundstories@gmail.com

Cover design by Linda Perry
Interior formatting by the authors

ISBN: 979-8-9999466-0-7
First edition, 2025
Printed in the United States of America

Also by the authors:
Poetry from the Heart: Searching for God in Everyday Life
Messages from the Mother (inspirational card deck)
"Sometimes we walk on holy ground without knowing it—until the
footprints behind us begin to glow."

Dedication

To all those who shared their stories—with honesty, with heart, with courage.

You trusted us with your moments of mystery, your glimpses of grace, your sacred ground.

This book exists because of you.

May your stories light the path for others.

May you always know:

You are not alone.

This book is a collection of holy moments, gathered from people of all ages, backgrounds, and beliefs.

Each story is a candle lit in darkness,

A reminder that the Divine meets us right where we are—

In ordinary shoes, on sacred ground.

"If you knew that whoever you meet has been sent by God, how would you treat them?"

—Alan Cohen

Editor's Note

When my friend, Linda, offered me the opportunity to edit this book, I was touched by her generosity. Little did I realize what a gift it would be.

Each of us faces times of difficulty, and this has been such a season for many. In these pages, I was reminded how graciously God enters our lives when we are most in need. Stories shared how little things can have outsized impacts, and grace forever abounds.

As you enter these pages, lay aside your preconceptions and let childlike openness lead you. Prepare to find Love's magic and be ready to embrace amazement.

This book is a gift for just such times as this one. Welcome to the blessing!

Always and Evermore,

JoAnn Jordan

Table of Contents

Introduction

After we published our first book, *Poetry From the Heart: Searching for God in Everyday Life*, something began to stir. We began to hear stories of how God—or the Divine—had touched lives. Sometimes in a subtle, quiet way. Sometimes in unmistakable, grand ones. People would share how God or someone else made a difference in their lives or how they had been that difference for someone else. And sometimes, we saw the ripple effects—set in motion by a single act of kindness.

Stories were filled with grace, with laughter, or with tears. Stories that inspired us. Stories that humbled us. Stories that blessed us.

Several times, we were told that telling the stories healed a part of them.

These stories needed to be honored, So we listened. We opened our hearts and our inboxes. What you hold in your hands is the result of that listening.

The title *Ordinary Shoes on Sacred Ground: There, God Was Also.* reflects the spirit of what we found. We walk through life thinking some moments are mundane. But when we pause, look closer, and really listen, we realize we're standing on sacred ground—every time compassion shows up, every time grace arrives uninvited, every time love speaks without words.

Sometimes, God touches our lives in dramatic ways—through healing, transformation, or miraculous encounters. But more often, it's in the smaller moments. A stranger's kindness. A sentence we didn't know we needed.

Just days before my own knee surgery, I met Sunita.

She was the RN who did my intake—asked the usual pre-op questions and drew my blood with a skill so gentle I barely felt the needle. But what I did feel was her presence.

On her wrist, I noticed a tattoo—like calligraphy. I asked her about it.

"It's my father's signature," she told me. "A gift to myself on Father's Day. His signature was in his prayer book." Then she smiled. "My father named me Sunita. It means sun. The light that shines on all."

She shared stories of her childhood in India and of her deep love for her father. "He was a very good man. He would always be teaching me. He always told me that when you go into a home—whether Hindu, Christian, Muslim, or Buddhist—you sprinkle blessings of God. There is no difference. We are all one."

As I was leaving, I thanked her for telling me about her father. She hugged me.

Everyone is a blessing. Sometimes, all it takes is someone else to bring it out.

That's what this book hopes to do: bring out the blessings we sometimes miss. Remind us that God doesn't need a grand stage. Just a willing heart and a pair of ordinary shoes walking on holy ground.

We gathered these stories one by one—from people ages 16 to 87, from different nations, faiths, and cultural backgrounds. Some identify with a specific religion; others do not. The stories span the full arc of life—offering glimpses of the sacred from before birth to beyond the grave. Some are dramatic. Some are subtle. But each one left us saying: *There, God was, also.*

We originally planned to include 111 stories—a number that symbolizes new beginnings and divine alignment. But the stories kept coming. So we extended our limit to 123, a number that carries its own spiritual rhythm: one, two, three… a sacred progression, a holy unfolding. And still, the stories continued. We finally realized—God doesn't stop at a given number, and neither will we.

We offer these stories as an invitation to notice the sacred in your own life.

May they bless you as they've blessed us.

In gratitude,

Joy LeChien & Linda Perry

Coauthors

1

Opening Blessing: The Thanksgiving Card's Adventure

Linda & Joy

For the past several years, Linda has painted seasonal scenes to turn into greeting cards for friends and loved ones. Each card is paired with a thoughtful poem and a handwritten message. Before mailing them, she holds the stack in her hands and whispers a blessing: "May Divine Love, which flows through me, bless and multiply peace and love to all who come in contact with these letters."

Last Thanksgiving, as always, cards were sent out. But one never arrived. A close friend, Joy, mentioned she hadn't received hers—until weeks later, long after Christmas had come and gone.

When she finally opened the envelope, something unexpected was tucked inside: a receipt from the IRS. Somehow, the card had ended up at an IRS facility in Ogden, Utah. Yet it had been addressed correctly to Arizona.

What happened between Texas and Arizona, we'll never know. But someone, somewhere—perhaps a weary government worker on a hard day—opened that envelope, read the Thanksgiving poem, and felt something shift. Maybe they smiled. Maybe they sighed. Maybe they felt seen or softened or steadied.

We believe the energy of kindness has a way of traveling to exactly where it's needed. Grace moves in ways we can't always predict. This simple card became something more than a mix-up—it became a reminder: love finds its way.

That is the spirit in which we offer this book. These stories are ordinary and extraordinary all at once. They carry the fingerprints of compassion, the scent of the sacred, and the surprise of grace. Like that wandering card, they're offered in faith and trust that they'll land in the right hands… maybe yours.

So, before you turn the page, we offer the same blessing to you: May Divine Love, which flows through these pages, bless and multiply peace and love to all who come in contact with these stories.

"You may not always see the result, but no act of love is ever lost."

— St. Teresa of Calcutta

2

Grace

This may be a simple question, but I was wondering about GRACE. What is it? Is it the same as God's love? Or is it an aspect of it?

I heard we are the Grace of God. So, how would the Grace of God "act"?

From a child, I was taught to sing Amazing Grace, then as a teenager, we sang the words to the tune of House of the Rising Sun. Back then, I thought it a bit more profound to sing it to the tune of House of the Rising Sun. Then in my Catholic years, we were encouraged to be in a "state of Grace", yet I never fully understood what the hell Grace is.

My youngest granddaughter's middle name is Grace, and so is one of our dogs. Neither one constantly "lives up" to its name. But is that not Grace?

I think I benefit from Grace, as when a friend comes and gives her time and energy in helping me clean out a closet or drawers.

I think I give Grace when I write a note of thanks to the server who brought me my meal and kept me in iced tea.

I think I witness glimpses of Grace, like last week, I saw two men at a corner, I assume both homeless. I called out to them and one approached the car. I gave him 4 one-dollar bills and told him that 2 of them were for his friend and the other 2 were his. He took the money and told me the man needed it much more than he did, and would give it all to him.

I'm reminded that many times I've heard, "There, but the Grace of God, go I". Where does it begin and end? Where does Grace not go?

I once heard that God's love can be explained like rocks in a river, where the water embraces all of them. Can that be said also of Grace?

Maybe the concept of Grace is to be elusive. But whatever it is, like the infinite love of God, grace may not be defined, and it is not an illusion.

"Grace is not part of consciousness: it is the amount of light in our souls, not knowledge or reason."

— Pope Francis

3

Living in the Moment: A Dog's Perspective

The other day, I watched our dog spin in delighted circles at the mention of a walk—as if this were the greatest joy he had ever known. And in that moment, I wondered: What if I lived like that?

We can find profound wisdom in a dog's love and companionship. While we're busy solving problems, chasing goals, or making ends meet, our dogs are simply present. They don't worry about outcomes. They don't rehash the past or dread the future. They just *are*—and they invite us into that same space.

Even when walking the same trail for the hundredth time, a dog experiences it like a new adventure. There is joy in their eyes over the simplest treat, exuberance in every step, and contentment when they curl up beside us. Their trust is whole. Their love, constant.

In those quiet moments—when their head rests in our lap or they sleep peacefully at our feet—we're reminded that we don't have to fix everything. We can simply *be*. We can breathe. We can love.

Maybe the key to a richer life isn't found in solving every problem, but in letting go—just enough—to feel the flow of life and love. Dogs remind us of that. They teach us how to live in the moment, not through words, but by presence.

And perhaps, through their simple, faithful joy, they are whispering a sacred truth:

This moment is enough.

> *"Be still and know that I am God."*
>
> *— Psalm 46:10 (NIV)*

4

The Cost of Everything, the Value of Nothing

I rest beneath a bridge while traffic rushes by overhead. No one notices me.

There was a time when I was known—and even feared. I drove luxury cars, wore Rolex watches and Armani suits, and dined on steak and wine. I thought I had everything.

Back then, I was climbing the corporate ladder—fast and ruthless. I didn't have time for friends or love. I hadn't seen my parents—hardworking, blue-collar folks—since I left for college. They lived only a few miles away, but I stayed away. I was too busy becoming someone important.

And then—just like that—it was gone.

The financial crash hit hard. My savings and 401(k)? Gone! My car was repossessed. I lost my high-rise apartment. I had no safety net. No one to call. Just me—and the fallout. I ended up homeless, hungry, invisible.

I remember standing in line at a soup kitchen for the first time, head down, ashamed. That's when I saw her—the administrative assistant I once fired. To this day, I can't remember why. She was there, filling water glasses and offering kind words to everyone. Her perfume was familiar, almost comforting. As she passed, she gently touched my hand, pretending not to recognize me. I couldn't meet her eyes. I couldn't speak. But I will never forget that moment.

A welfare worker came over and offered help. I didn't even know what to say. I just nodded—and for the first time in years, I cried. Not just for what I'd lost, but for who I had become. That was the beginning.

He helped me enroll in a program that provided meals, support, and job opportunities. They taught me how to hammer a nail—how to build homes for others. And maybe, in the process, rebuild myself.

Days turned into weeks, weeks into months, then years. The ambition I once poured into corporate gain softened into something deeper: compassion. Now, I drive an old F-150 and work with Habitat for Humanity, building homes for people I once looked down on.

And I fell in love—with a single mom of three. At 5:30 p.m., you'll find me with a kid on my lap, a dog at my side, helping with homework or dinner. Saturday mornings, we watch cartoons. Sundays, we make waffles. These are the memories I cherish now.

I still volunteer at the soup kitchen—the same one where I once received grace I didn't deserve. Now I'm the one who smiles, who listens, who fills the plates.

There was a night, early on, when I sat on a cot in a shelter and whispered a prayer. I didn't even know what to say—just that I was empty. I didn't think God heard people like me. But He did. I see that now.

Not all at once. But little by little, He began putting the pieces back together. Letting me break, so He could rebuild me into someone better. Sometimes I think about calling my dad. Maybe I will—tomorrow.

But today... today, I'm living a life I never thought I'd have. A life money could never buy—and grace freely given.

"I once was lost, but now am found; was blind, but now I see."

— John Newton

5

Jury Duty: Diversity Coming Together

A letter from the city arrived, and it wasn't one I expected. I had been officially summoned for jury duty. As I read through the details, I caught myself searching for a clause—*any* clause—that might disqualify me. But no luck. I met all the criteria, and so I would be participating. I reminded myself that jury duty is both a legal and civic responsibility, and that only about 5% of people actually end up serving on a jury.

When I checked in, I was given a numbered badge—#32 in a group of 50—and directed to a small, somewhat cramped room that reminded me of an airport waiting area, but dedicated to civic duty. Some people were glued to their phones, others flipped through books or chatted in low voices.

What struck me most was the diversity in the room. People of all ages—young adults barely 18 to seniors in their 70s. Every race, likely all kinds of religious backgrounds or none at all. Some wore business suits, others were in work boots and utility gear. We were strangers, each from our own corner of the city, yet summoned to the same place for the same purpose.

After about thirty minutes, we were called to line up in numerical order and pass through a metal detector into the courtroom. Once inside, the judge addressed us. He reminded us of a foundational principle of our justice system: that every person is presumed innocent until proven guilty. It was a good reminder—one that extends beyond the courtroom into our everyday lives.

The case on the docket was a traffic violation. To my surprise, the defendant believed she did not need to show proof of a driver's license while driving a car with an expired registration. During the proceedings, the judge asked if anyone was 70 or older and offered them the chance to be excused. Several hands went up, and each person declined the opportunity to sit out. Not a single person accepted the offer. Their quiet willingness to stay spoke volumes.

In the end, I wasn't chosen as one of the jurors. Still, the day stayed with me. It reminded me that even in the ordinary moments, showing up matters. We complain about jury duty, but it's how the wheels of justice keep turning—through the willingness of everyday people to come together. No, it wasn't the highlight of my week. But it was the right thing to do.

"Let justice roll on like a river, righteousness like a never-failing stream."

— Amos 5:24

6

The Assignment I Didn't See

A few years ago, I left a stable job, thinking I was being guided to return to teaching. Early in my new position, my supervisor told me about her elderly mother, who had just moved into the area and needed help getting groceries. I referred her to the organization I had previously worked for, which helps seniors with shopping and other support services.

Ironically, I soon realized that returning to teaching wasn't right for me—it was overwhelming for many reasons. I found myself back at my old job not long after.

Then one day, I received a call from my former boss. She told me that during the intake process for her mother, it was determined she needed a product called a GAP (Guardian Angel Protection)—a bracelet or necklace with a button that can be pressed in case of emergency.

Her mother received the unit. That very night, while in the shower, she began bleeding profusely from a vein—something related to a medical condition. If she hadn't had that GAP device, she would have died. But because she had it, she received help in time.

I suddenly realized that maybe the entire reason I didn't return to that job, however briefly, was to save this woman's life. Had I not mentioned the program when I did, she wouldn't have received the device in time.

That experience shifted my perspective. What I had seen as a misstep or failure—leaving a stable job and starting a new one—was, in truth, a divine assignment. I was in the exact place I needed to be, for someone else's miracle.

This experience also reminded me how harsh we can be with ourselves. We often can't see the whole picture. But what feels like the "wrong" thing might actually be the very path through which love flows.

As the world becomes more fragmented, I've noticed how afraid people are to connect. In Nashville, I saw people apologizing for tiny things, afraid of being too much or not enough. We're forgetting we are one. And that's what A Course in Miracles says is our greatest problem—*separation.*

But even in that fear, love finds a way. And I'll never forget that my small action helped save a life. What I thought was a mistake turned out to be a miracle.

"You cannot know the outcome which is best. And so you trust it all to One who does."

— A Course in Miracles

7

A Journey of the Heart

I moved to Georgia in the late '90s and co-owned a coffee shop called Java Joe's. That's where I met my husband—he owned the building where my shop was located. As time went on, we got to know each other, began dating, and eventually married.

His parents welcomed me with open arms. His mother, especially, treated me like a daughter. Over time, my father-in-law passed away, and my husband and I made a big decision: we purchased ten acres and an old Victorian home, with a cabin out back for my mother-in-law. She was getting older, and it felt like the right thing to do.

She lived to be 94. During those years, we enjoyed puzzles, gardening, and quiet afternoons together. I took her to church and doctor appointments. I loved her dearly.

After she passed, things between my husband and me grew strained. Managing such a large property became overwhelming. But then my sister said something I'll never forget. She told me, "After she passed, I didn't know what she would have done without you. God sent her an angel."

Her words gave me peace.

I no longer regret buying the house or taking on the responsibility. Instead, I feel deeply grateful. I had the privilege of loving and caring for a beautiful soul in her final years. I miss her. I love her still.

"There are angels who walk this earth, disguised as daughters-in-law."

— Author unknown

8

Garden Intruder

On a beautiful spring afternoon, I was sitting peacefully in my flower garden when I noticed my neighbor's black cat wandering through the blossoms. It stopped, locked eyes with me, and began meowing in clear protest. The message was unmistakable: *You don't belong here.*

I couldn't help but laugh. This little cat was so certain that *I* was the intruder—in my own sanctuary.

But as I watched it flick its tail and strut among the flowers, a deeper reflection began to bloom. How often do *I* perceive the Divine as the intruder in *my* life?

When circumstances shift or routines get disrupted, I sometimes react like that cat—guarding my space, resisting change, and forgetting that everything, including this garden, ultimately belongs to God. Each plant, insect, and wandering creature has its role in a delicate, divinely orchestrated balance.

Perhaps moments of discomfort aren't intrusions at all—but invitations. Invitations to recognize that I'm part of something far greater, something sacred. God's divine tapestry, woven through soil and petal, meow and silence, is always beckoning me to engage more fully with the world around me.

And sometimes, it takes a small black cat to remind me.

"The earth is the Lord's, and everything in it, the world, and all who live in it."

— Psalm 24:1

9

Numbers of the Heart

When my mother passed away, I became unreachable—walled off from the world in a way I couldn't explain. My heart had closed. I went through the motions of daily life, but I felt like no one really cared. Even people of faith seemed distant. I started to believe something must be wrong with me, yet I kept pushing forward, asking for nothing, just trying to survive.

At the same time, I was caring for my husband, who was battling Alzheimer's and dementia, all while commuting forty miles each day to work in downtown Nashville. I was exhausted in every possible way—emotionally, spiritually, physically.

Not long after Mama's passing—maybe even the first night—I got up in the middle of the night and glanced at the clock: it read "1:11." The next night, I saw "2:22." Then came "3:33." I couldn't explain it, but each number stirred something in me. I began to wonder: *Was someone trying to reach me?*

Maybe it was my mother. Maybe it was God. Whatever it was, it reached me in a way no words could.

I didn't share this with many people. I knew some might think it was crazy. But I kept seeing the numbers: "4:44," then "5:55." Eventually, I looked into it and learned about angel numbers. Even though I've always been a skeptic—maybe even a "doubting Thomas"—I felt strangely comforted. If there was a message coming through, whoever was sending it clearly knew how to get my attention.

That's when something shifted. I didn't need others to understand. What mattered was that, somehow, I finally knew:

I was not alone.

"Indeed, the very hairs of your head are all numbered. Don't be afraid; you are worth more than many sparrows."

— Luke 12:7

10

Miracles Still Happen

A miracle that resonates deeply with me happened in 2020, the moment I was diagnosed with breast cancer.

Just before receiving the news, I had scheduled a session with a friend who practices spiritual healing. During our time together, he was drawn to my breast area and focused his healing energy there. His intuition prompted me to follow up with a mammogram.

The first mammogram revealed a lump. I was referred for a second one at the hospital for confirmation. But something astonishing happened—by the time I went for the hospital scan, before any treatment had begun, the lump had already shrunk by a full centimeter.

The contrast between the two mammograms was undeniable. I knew, deep in my being, that healing had already begun—physically, spiritually, and beyond what any medical chart could explain.

Throughout my cancer journey, I continued embracing spiritual healing. I leaned into my connection with Christ. During meditation and dreams, Jesus reassured me: *You are ready for this. It is time for your healing.*

Now, four years later, I am joyfully cancer-free. But more than that, I've awakened to the living presence of Christ within me. That inner knowing, that sacred guidance, is what truly carried me through.

"He said to her, 'Daughter, your faith has healed you. Go in peace and be freed from your suffering.'"

— Mark 5:34

11

Holy Moments: Journey Through Life and Death

There was a time in my life when several people I transported—or had become friends with—were nearing the end of their lives. I didn't always know their circumstances, only that they seemed drawn to me. Somehow, they wanted to connect.

One of those people was an elderly holy man with whom I formed an especially deep bond. He taught me a great deal in a short time, and his influence was instrumental in leading me to visit Yogananda's ashram in Encinitas, California. Our time together was brief—he was ill, and he passed away soon after.

These intense encounters with people close to death began to stir something in me. I realized this wasn't a coincidence; it was calling. I enrolled in a Death Doula course and began exploring one of what I believe are my many purposes.

Recently, I began volunteering with hospice. In this space of quiet service, I've come to see death not as an ending, but as a sacred transition. Being with people in that liminal time has brought me peace and clarity.

A few months after starting, I was present during the final hours of my best friend's life. As I prayed beside her, I felt the unmistakable presence of the Holy Spirit in the room. It was as if the Divine whispered, *You are exactly where you're meant to be.*

That moment solidified what my soul already knew: I had found a sacred place of service, a calling that brings deep peace and spiritual purpose—not just to others, but to me as well.

"There is no death because the Son of God is like his Father. Nothing you can do can change Eternal Love."

— A Course in Miracles

12

Found in Pages

I recently went through several journals from five years ago, and I was shocked at what I found. My thoughts back then were tangled in confusion, darkness, and despair. It felt like reading the pages of someone who was lost at sea.

Now, five years later, I'm physically back in the same place I left—after having spent four and a half years immersed in the awakening power of Sedona. And I'll admit, the ego tried to tell me I had gained nothing. That I had regressed. That all the healing and growth had evaporated.

But those journals? They told a different story. They told the truth.

Reading those old entries, I realized how far I've come. I am no longer plagued by those dark, chaotic thoughts. I've reclaimed my soul. I know who I am, and I know how I want to live: fully committed to doing God's will—whatever that looks like.

Then there's my best friend, my ex-husband. Five years ago, he was closed off, hardened, and didn't believe God even existed. Today, he's asking to know Jesus. We're going to watch the new episodes of *The Chosen* together at the IMAX. That's a miracle I didn't see coming.

I'm grateful that I went looking for a story in those journals—because what I found was myself. Not the version I once hoped to be, polished and shining in a place where everyone thinks they're enlightened. No. I found my light right here, in a world that *needs* it.

We're in this together—all of us. And I will carry that truth with me until my final breath…and into whatever comes next.

"The soul always knows what to do to heal itself. The challenge is to silence the mind."

— Caroline Myss

13

The Gift of Awareness

One day I was in Flagstaff, waiting for a client to come out of her orthopedic appointment. I was parked facing the building when I noticed a woman walking toward her car. I could see that she was in a lot of pain. I didn't feel called to approach her—instead, I quietly sent her love and compassion from where I sat.

She got into the car parked next to me, rolled down her window, and said, "Hi! Beautiful." I wasn't surprised. It felt like a very natural exchange in that moment. I told her I had seen the pain she was in, and she went on to tell me about her condition. I responded with kindness, wishing her healing and bridging the moment with understanding.

A little while later, she rolled down her window again and called out, "Goodbye, Beautiful, and God bless." I smiled and replied, "God bless," back to her.

That brief connection confirmed something to me: when we send love to others, something in their soul receives it. That day, I was blessed to receive a small miracle in return—one that now inspires me to bless anyone or any place I feel called to silently.

This moment could have passed unnoticed, but I believe God placed her in my view so that both of us could feel seen and supported. This was holy in the simplest way.

"We shall never know all the good that a simple smile can do."

— Mother Teresa

14

God's GPS

The last time we drove home to Wisconsin from Sedona, we drove straight through—1,734 miles in about 26 hours. There were four of us, so we took turns behind the wheel. I ended up driving the last six hours of the trip.

Now, I've never really liked driving in heavy traffic, and I realized we'd be hitting Madison, Wisconsin's beltline, right at rush hour. As we got closer, I started to feel anxious. I whispered a prayer: "God, You know I don't like driving in this kind of traffic. I'm getting nervous. Please be with me. Let me feel Your peace as I go through this."

Not even two miles later, the GPS announced, "There's an alternate route up ahead."

I figured, "Why not?" and took the exit. The new route took us around the outskirts of Madison on beautiful, winding, hilly country roads. It only added about ten minutes to the trip—and after 24 hours of driving, what's ten more minutes?

We've traveled this route many times, and that alternate path has never shown up before. Maybe it wasn't a miracle in the traditional sense, but I know in my heart: God answered my prayer. He gave me peace, and He gave me beauty. That detour turned what could've been a stressful stretch into a joyful one.

And for that, I'm grateful.

"Trust in the Lord with all your heart and lean not on your own understanding; in all your ways submit to him, and he will make your paths straight."

— Proverbs 3:5-6

15

Unexpected Connections

In a previous job, I was occasionally assigned to drive two people to the same appointment, often over a long distance. On one particular day, when I saw the two names on my list, I felt a sense of dread. I silently began to pray, preparing myself for what I expected to be a challenging trip.

But something unexpected happened.

As we drove, the two passengers began to talk—and to my surprise, they quickly discovered they had much in common. The car filled with warmth and laughter, and what I had feared would be a long, uncomfortable journey transformed into something beautiful.

By the end of the trip, they exchanged phone numbers. I got to witness a genuine connection blossom right there in my backseat. It reminded me that we never really know how our day will unfold—and for that, I am grateful.

What began with apprehension ended with joy. The experience reminded me to stay open to the moments I don't expect. God knows what He's doing—even when I don't.

"Love is the bridge between you and everything."

— Rumi

16

Helping Kids Find Their Way

I recently started working for a company similar to Lyft or Uber, but focused on driving people to their medical appointments. One afternoon, I was transporting a woman home when she began talking about a driver she'd had in the past—someone who used to transport children to and from school. She seemed surprised to learn that it was actually a formal service.

As she spoke, something clicked. I told her that I used to do that exact work about four years ago. She mentioned that the program might need drivers again. That evening, I decided to look into it—and within ten minutes, I had the job. The whole thing happened so fast it made my head spin.

That small conversation, with someone I'd been randomly assigned to drive, turned out to be a doorway. It led me toward more stable income, yes—but even more than that, it opened up a new opportunity to serve. I'll be transporting children who have been displaced from their homes, helping them get to the schools they're familiar with.

I'm looking forward to spending time with the kids—connecting with them, and also reconnecting with my own inner child, who could use a bit more joy and playfulness during this time of transition. I hope to offer each child not just a safe ride, but a moment of care, support, and maybe even laughter along the way.

"Sometimes a seemingly random moment is the answer to a prayer you didn't know you were praying."

— Unknown

17

Rose-scented Guidance

I called a client who needed a ride to the dentist. She sounded confused and had trouble telling me her address. Before I left to pick her up, I prayed—to be of service without becoming enmeshed, to be a bridge, and to be a vessel of love and light.

As we drove to the dentist's office, I suddenly noticed the undeniable scent of roses filling the car. I asked her if she smelled them. She replied simply, "I love roses."

In that moment, I silently asked Mother Mary what she wanted me to do.

When we arrived, the client asked for my phone number so she could call me when her appointment was over. I gently told her that I was only assigned to drop her off and that she could call the transport number for her return ride. But she said she didn't know the number. I gave her my number anyway and contacted my supervisor. I was told she would need to call the number on the back of her Medicare card—but an hour later, she called me again to say she didn't have the card with her.

I decided to return and drive her home, even though I wouldn't be compensated. When I checked my location, I realized I was already just five minutes away, after having driven around for an hour.

On the way home, she spoke about how people need to be kind to each other and told me that she watches "God's shows" all day long. When we arrived, she thanked me for being kind.

I was grateful—not only to be of service, but to feel that Mother Mary had been in the car with us that day, her presence wrapped in rose-scented grace.

"If you ever feel overwhelmed, remember that even roses grow in thorns."

— Unknown

18

Forgiveness Sees a Cry for Love

All my life, I've done a pretty good job of loving people, putting myself in their shoes, and avoiding judgment. But there was one person who challenged that part of me. I kept hearing negative stories about her from different people—how she was controlling, unkind, even a bully. When someone close to me was deeply hurt by her, I began to fall into the trap of hating her, even though she had never wronged me directly.

That hatred didn't sit right with me. It wasn't who I was. I knew I had to take a different path, so I chose forgiveness.

To my surprise, this same individual has recently become an encouraging presence in my life—something I hadn't experienced from anyone else in quite the same way. Through attending her classes, I've learned powerful lessons about truth and self-worth. She helped me see that no person is better than another—a truth that touched me deeply, as I've often struggled with feeling "less than," no matter how much I've achieved.

I'm grateful that I was able to shift my perception of her. What I once saw as harshness or ego, I now recognize as a cry for love.

This journey hasn't just healed my view of her—it has helped me deepen compassion for myself and for others. Forgiveness, I've learned, is often the key to freeing our hearts from judgment and returning to love.

"Every loving thought is true. Everything else is a cry for healing and help, regardless of the form it takes."

— A Course in Miracles

19

Beyond the Wreckage

It was the day after St. Patrick's Day, and I was headed to work. The car in front of me suddenly hit the cement divider wall and flipped over. I pulled over, called 911, and saw that one of the people in the car had been ejected. I ran to him, but it was too late—he was already gone. Another passenger was still trapped inside, and I managed to get him out quickly.

By that time, other good Samaritans had also stopped to help. One of them suggested we move out of the street. Just as we stepped to the side of the road, a drunk driver crashed into my car and completely demolished it. I had been standing in that exact spot just seconds before.

As I stood beside the wreckage, I was struck by how quickly life can change. That day reminded me of the fragility of existence—and the importance of showing up for others in their moments of need. My car was destroyed, but I walked away unharmed, a living reminder that our paths are often guided by something greater.

I went to work expecting a routine morning. Instead, I found purpose. Sometimes, it's in the wreckage that we find our strength.

"Perhaps this is the moment for which you have been created."

— Esther 4:14

20

Grace In a Fall

My elderly mom lives alone in another city. Not long ago, she fell and broke several ribs. It was a painful experience — and yet, I truly believe it turned out to be a blessing in disguise.

While she was in the ER, the doctors discovered something they might never have seen otherwise: she had an aneurysm. It could have ended in tragedy, but because of that fall, she received the surgery she needed and spent time in the ICU recovering.

Once she regained her strength, the plan was to send her to rehab. But unexpectedly, she didn't qualify. At first, this felt like a setback — but in hindsight, I see it as another piece of divine intervention.

Instead of going to a facility, my mom was able to stay with her sister — who, on the very day of my mom's fall, had just lost her husband while he was in hospice care.

That unexpected turn brought deep blessings to both women. They were able to support each other through grief and healing, sharing companionship in a moment of profound need. The loneliness they might have faced separately was softened by the presence of each other.

I truly believe God had a hand in all of it — guiding my mom to a place of care and comfort, and offering my aunt unexpected companionship in her hour of sorrow. It's remarkable how the pieces fell into place, and I remain deeply grateful for the quiet ways God has been present in our family's journey through this difficult season.

"Even in the brokenness, there is blessing."

— Morgan Harper Nichols

21

Tides of Courage

We were on vacation at South Padre Island, enjoying some quality time with our three children. One sunny day, we decided to head to the beach. But our first stop didn't sit well with my wife—she said it was, in her words, "too people-y." So, we moved on. The next beach wasn't right either; "It just doesn't feel right," she said. At the third stop, her disappointment grew: "There's litter everywhere."

By this point, I was getting frustrated. We had only one beach left to try. Thankfully, this one met her standards—she deemed it "acceptable."

As we set up our umbrella and unpacked floaty toys, my wife spotted a family in the water. She thought they were yelling for help. I assumed they were playing. Never underestimate your wife's intuition.

She sprang into action. She told our oldest to go find help and warned the younger kids in a tone that left no room for debate: "Do *not* go near the water." Then she rushed into the waves. I hesitated—paralyzed by fear. What if I drowned and left our children without a father? But watching my wife run toward the danger left me no choice. I had to follow her.

In the water, we found a man struggling to hold his wife's head above the waves while trying to cling to his children. The current was strong, and although we were less than a foot away, we couldn't reach them.

Neither my wife nor I is a strong swimmer, but we were determined not to let them drown. Thankfully, the man our oldest son had alerted showed up just in time. He was tall enough to reach the woman and handed her to my wife while I helped the children. Together, we pulled the family to shore. The woman was coughing up water but regained consciousness.

Meanwhile, our children had been little heroes of their own. The son of the man who came to help had tried to run into the waves after his dad. Our kids stopped him and said, "If we can't go in, you can't either."

As the chaos subsided, a small crowd of concerned beachgoers gathered around. Physically and emotionally drained, we packed up and left. But as we reflected on what had happened, we knew deep in our hearts: we had been led to that beach for a reason.

"Be strong and courageous. Do not be afraid; do not be discouraged, for the Lord your God will be with you wherever you go."

— Joshua 1:9

22

Traveling from Panic to Peace

A few years ago, I planned my first Christmas trip to Kansas City in four years and was excited to spend time with my family. I normally relied on a hotel shuttle to get to the airport, but this time, my usual option was unavailable. I found another motel with what I assumed was shuttle service—but I hadn't read the fine print.

When I arrived, I discovered there was no shuttle at all. Panic set in. I was told it might be difficult to find a ride, especially on short notice. I paused, took a deep breath, and asked for help—out loud and inwardly. Then I walked outside, hoping for a solution.

Just then, I noticed a couple who had just ordered an Uber. When I explained my situation, they kindly offered to share their ride. Relief washed over me.

But once we got to the airport, another wave of stress hit: the line was long, and I was running out of time. The airline had a strict cutoff for check-in, and I was cutting it close. I tried the kiosk, but it didn't work. I rushed to the counter to explain everything. The agent wasn't sure he could get me on the flight and warned it might cost extra. I didn't hesitate—I told him, "I don't care what it costs. I just want to be with my family."

After a tense moment, he printed my ticket. I nearly cried with gratitude.

That day reminded me how easily fear can cloud our view—and how quickly grace can clear it. When things go wrong, it's tempting to spiral. But if we pause, ask for help, and stay centered, support often shows up in the most unexpected ways. I was never truly alone on that journey. And neither are you.

"Faith is taking the first step even when you don't see the whole staircase."

— Martin Luther King Jr.

23

Divinely Guided Airport Assistance

A few years ago, I was flying back to Kansas City from Chicago, with a connecting flight to Denver.

My flight to Denver was delayed, and as I waited at the airport, I quietly began reciting the Serenity Prayer. It helped keep me calm as the clock ticked on.

When we finally landed in Denver, I got a notification that my next flight was boarding. I looked around at the crowded plane and felt a rising sense of urgency. Without even thinking, I began the Serenity Prayer again.

And that's when things started to shift.

Somehow, I managed to exit the plane faster than expected. The crowd seemed to part at just the right moments, almost as if I were being gently guided through.

As I reached the terminal, a man in a motorized cart suddenly pulled up beside me. "Need a ride?" he asked.

Grateful, I nodded, and he motioned for me to hop on. As we sped toward my gate, he turned and asked, "Is your name Woolford?"

I blinked in surprise. "Yes," I said.

To this day, I have no idea how he knew my name. Maybe he overheard it. Maybe someone called ahead. Maybe something greater was at work.

As we pulled up, I saw the gate agent just beginning to close the door. I made it onto the plane—*just in time.*

That day felt nothing short of miraculous. I believe I was being looked after, moment by moment. And I was reminded that prayer is not just a plea—it's a way to steady our spirit and invite grace into the moment.

> *"I am sustained by the Love of God."*
>
> *— A Course in Miracles*

24

Power of Kindness

I've worked in the restaurant business for as long as I can remember. Most days, my work starts at 6:30 a.m., brewing coffee and tea at a café that serves breakfast and lunch.

The morning crowd is usually made up of regulars who order the same thing every day. I try to have their drinks waiting on the table where they like to sit.

But that day, everything felt off. Some of the guys at the "old codger's table" got into a heated argument. My co-worker was out with COVID, my feet and back were aching, and two tables had left without leaving a tip.

To top it off, I knew I'd be working late. My co-worker usually helped with cleanup while I wrapped utensils in napkins for the next day. Now, both jobs fell to me. I was already tired, and the shift wasn't even over.

Just before closing, an older lady came in. I greeted her with a forced smile, silently thinking, *"Oh no... older folks sometimes take a long time to eat, and we can't start cleaning until everyone's gone."* But she smiled back and kindly asked how my day was going. Then, to my surprise, she ordered quickly and only ate a few bites before asking for a takeout box. After she left, I found a note on her table—along with a generous tip.

The note read:

"Thank you for being my server today. I know this job is not easy—being on your feet all day, dealing with different types of people, and smiling even when it's tough. But you really DO make a difference, even if no one notices or returns your smile. Thank you again. Many blessings."

Reading those words brought tears to my eyes. She saw me—not just as a server, but as a person. That small act of kindness turned my whole day around.

I hadn't seen her since—not for two years. I often wondered what had happened to her. Then, last week, she walked in with her husband. I said, "I remember you!" and pulled out the yellowed note I had saved all this time. I showed it to her. She was surprised I had kept it. I told her I read it whenever I'm having a rough day. She smiled and said, "Well then, you just made *my* day."

"Therefore encourage one another and build each other up, just as in fact you are doing."

— 1 Thessalonians 5:11

25

A Stroke of Destiny

Several years ago, when my husband was still alive, his mother—whom I adored—lived about two hours away from us. She was in her 80s but in remarkably good health.

One night, Rick, a close friend of ours, was driving home from work. He knew my mother-in-law well but hadn't seen her in years.

All of a sudden, he felt a strong, undeniable urge to turn his car around and visit her.

When he arrived at her house, they sat down to catch up. But during their conversation, Rick noticed something strange—her speech began to slur, and she wasn't acting like herself.

Something was clearly wrong. Rick didn't hesitate. He called 911.

Thanks to his quick thinking, the paramedics arrived in time to discover she was having a stroke. Because of Rick's decision to stop by, she received immediate medical care—and it saved her life.

We truly believe he was guided by a higher power that night.

After the stroke, my mother-in-law came home and began physical therapy. She made a full recovery and went on to live another eight beautiful years.

There's no doubt in my heart—she had angels watching over her that night.

"The steps of a good man are ordered by the Lord: and he delighteth in his way."

— Psalm 37:23

26

Smuggled Grace

I'd like to share a story about the time I brought some Bibles into an Eastern European country under communist control, back in 1975.

As I was preparing to leave Dallas, someone gifted me a fortune-telling book from *Cosmopolitan* magazine. I smiled, thanked them, and tucked it into my carry-on bag—right on top of about thirty small, pocket-sized Bibles I had packed to bring with me.

At the time, the country I was traveling to was under strict communist rule, and the possession or distribution of Bibles was illegal. I knew the risk, but felt strongly that I was meant to bring them.

When I arrived, I had to pass through customs. Officers were inspecting luggage carefully and confiscating anything they deemed inappropriate. My heart pounded as I approached the inspection area. Quietly, I began to pray.

As they searched my carry-on, they immediately spotted the fortune-telling book. The officers took it out, exchanged amused glances, and laughed. "Crazy American," they muttered. Then, to my amazement, they put the book back in the bag—never even looking beneath it—and waved me through.

I passed through customs, completely unaware that I had just avoided what could have been very serious consequences.

Looking back, I have no doubt that I was protected by a higher power. That experience affirmed for me that God has a plan for each and every one of us—even when we're holding nothing but a prayer and a bag full of hope.

"The Lord will rescue me from every evil attack and will bring me safely to his heavenly kingdom."

— 2 Timothy 4:18

27

Angels of the Haunted House

About nine years ago, I began writing a novel inspired by a vivid dream. The story involved ghosts, so I searched online for real haunted houses in the United States to help set the atmosphere. I eventually found one in a small Indiana town that seemed perfect. I studied its layout and used it as a model to describe various rooms in my story.

Five years later, while planning a visit to Bloomington, Indiana, to see my niece in college, the memory of that haunted house suddenly returned. I had completely forgotten about it. After a little brainstorming, the name came back to me.

To my surprise, a quick search revealed it was only about 30 miles from where I'd be staying.

Excited, I told my niece about it, and we decided to go see the house. I took several photos while we were there, including one I later sent to a friend—an artist—who used it as the inspiration for a painting. That painting became the cover of my book.

What struck me most about the house were the **two angels** on either side of the staircase leading to the front porch. I hadn't remembered them from my original research, but there they were—standing as guardians, peaceful and present.

Around the same time, my life was beginning to shift. I discovered a spiritual community in Sedona, Arizona, led by a teacher whose work spoke deeply to me. I eventually moved there for a while, and it became a kind of pilgrimage—one of self-discovery, healing, and spiritual growth.

Looking back, I can see how these moments were part of something greater—how stories, symbols, places, and people were divinely woven into my journey.

Sometimes, we don't recognize how carefully orchestrated our lives are until much later. But there is a higher power at work—always guiding, always blessing, always desiring our happiness.

"Coincidence is God's way of remaining anonymous."

— Albert Einstein

28

Angels on the Interstate

One day, I was driving two clients to their doctor's appointments in Flagstaff. We were traveling on a major highway when, just a few car lengths ahead in the opposite lane, I noticed a truck.

Suddenly, a ladder flew out of the back of that truck—bouncing and tumbling across the road—coming straight toward us.

In that moment, I instinctively prayed for guidance.

I slammed on the brakes. The client in the back seat gasped, startled. But somehow, there were no cars directly behind me—and none to my left.

The ladder hit the pavement just short of our car. I was able to safely steer around it, still driving, still steady.

When I glanced in the rearview mirror, I saw other cars slowing and swerving, miraculously avoiding it as well.

What struck me most was the overwhelming peace I felt. It was as if time had slowed down. I wasn't afraid. There was no panic—only clarity.

Later, the client in the front seat wrote a letter to my boss, praising my quick thinking and calm response.

But I know it wasn't just me.

I believe my angels were with me—guiding, protecting, clearing the way.

They were there when I called.

They always are.

"He will cover you with his feathers, and under his wings you will find refuge; his faithfulness will be your shield and rampart."

— Psalm 91:4

29

Carried By Love

During the height of COVID, one of my closest friends was diagnosed with brain cancer. It was discovered during a workup for a fall and changes in her mental status.

Her doctor called to tell me while I was out of town on a family vacation.

Though she had lived here for 35 years, her home was England—and all her family was there. She could no longer travel alone due to her physical and cognitive decline, and her family was desperate to bring her home to care for her during her final days.

I sat in my car on the beach and began making calls—dozens, then hundreds. No one had a solution. I prayed that God would find a way. My very last call was to the British embassy. They explained that although it could take weeks to approve emergency visas with quarantine requirements, there *was* a path forward: if we accompanied her on the flight and didn't go through customs ourselves, we could turn around and fly back to the U.S. the same day without quarantining.

That was our way.

I left my family vacation, and two days later, another dear friend and I boarded a flight with her to England. She had always had an intense fear of flying. But this time, because of the cancer, she didn't even realize she was on a plane. She was calm, peaceful—held by something beyond understanding.

When we landed in London, flight attendants wheeled her through customs to where her family was waiting. As we watched her cross over into their care, we broke down sobbing.

We knew we would never see her again. And still—we were thankful. Thankfully, we were able to bring her home.

I will always be grateful for the peace God gave her mind. She had long feared being incapacitated or becoming dependent on others. And although those fears came to pass, *she never felt them.*

God, in His mercy, sheltered her. She never even knew she had cancer. All she knew, in the end, was the love and comfort of her family. She passed away peacefully two months later.

"You will keep in perfect peace those whose minds are steadfast, because they trust in you."

— Isaiah 26:3

30

Clearing the Road for Love

Every late spring, in a rural part of Dutchess County, New York, a painful pattern seemed to repeat itself: a teenager fatally injured in a car accident.

It had gone on for several years. Eight years ago, the victim was my son-in-law's cousin's son. The year after, it was the brother of my granddaughter's friend. Each spring brought fresh sorrow—and I began to feel a spiritual call to do something.

As a Reiki Master and a social worker, I've conducted many energy clearings—at private homes and even in nursing home rooms. I believe in addressing suffering on both the emotional and energetic levels. This time, I felt drawn to the land itself.

I approached Loretta, a nurse at the nursing home where I worked, and asked if she'd join me. Though we had never done spiritual work together before, she was someone I trusted and knew would bring a grounded, caring presence.

Before our planned meeting, Loretta told me she had something to share. When we met, she revealed that her own daughter had died in a car accident years earlier—at just sixteen. I hadn't known. Even more astonishing, the accident had happened on the very road where we would be gathering.

The connection was undeniable. We both knew we were being called to something greater. Loretta suggested we invite her friend Veronica, a channeler, who agreed to join us. We began our mission at the local high school. In the parking lot, Veronica channeled the spirit of a young man who had died while driving his grandfather's pickup truck—back in 1947. His energy had remained in the area, perhaps influencing or attracting other tragedies.

We performed a clearing there, then moved on to two roads where the more recent fatal accidents had occurred. In each place, we offered prayer and light.

That was nearly seven years ago. And since then, not one teenager has died in a car accident on those roads.

Every time I perform a clearing, I begin with a prayer to the Archangels—calling them by name. I ask for help in freeing any lingering spirits, so they can move on to where they truly belong. It's all done with love. Always.

"Blessed are the peacemakers, for they will be called children of God."

— Matthew 5:9

31

Mother's Love Through Son's Recovery

It was a calm Sunday morning. I was watching church on TV, and everything felt peaceful—until the phone rang.

The news shattered everything: my 21-year-old son had been shot, and the doctors didn't believe he would survive.

It was a dumb kid's accident. His best friend since the 8th grade was holding a gun. Thinking the chamber was empty, she pulled the trigger.

The bullet struck him in the center of his chest. It grazed his heart, tore through his liver, pancreas, and diaphragm, and lodged near the aorta of his left kidney before exiting through his back.

He underwent three surgeries.

When my son finally woke up, his first concern wasn't for himself—it was for his friend.

Throughout it all, I remained calm, and I can only credit that to my faith in God. It grounded me through those long, terrifying weeks.

The recovery process was incredibly difficult. My vibrant, energetic son now moved like an elderly man. He battled PTSD—something he hid from most people. But I saw it. I sat with him in the night through his fears and nightmares.

Bit by bit, he began to heal.

He eventually became a paralegal and is now continuing his education to become a lawyer.

All charges against his friend were dropped. I've chosen to forgive her, but I will never forget what happened—and she is no longer welcome in my home.

Some things I may never fully understand. But I trust God has a purpose for my son's life. I believe he will go on to make a powerful difference in this world.

"Many are the plans in a person's heart, but it is the Lord's purpose that prevails."

— Proverbs 19:21

32

My Guardian Angel Works Overtime

About twelve years ago, my husband and I were involved in a serious car accident—hit head-on by a drunk driver. When the insurance adjusters reviewed the wreckage, they told us we shouldn't have survived.

My husband came through with only bruises and a concussion. I was not so fortunate. I suffered a severe spinal injury. Doctors told me surgery couldn't fix it, and specialists warned I might never walk again.

At the time, I could barely use my arms. My husband had to lift me from my chair to move me anywhere. I was overwhelmed—not just by pain, but by anger and bitterness.

Still, I refused to give up. I worked tirelessly, and after a long, difficult recovery, I did regain the ability to walk. My balance isn't perfect, but I'm walking—and that alone is a miracle.

I've always loved plants, and my sunroom is filled with them. Rows and rows of them sit on shelves. One day, I knew they needed water, and though I couldn't reach the top ones safely, I didn't want to wait.

Ignoring my better judgment, I climbed onto a step stool with the watering can in hand. As I reached upward, I lost my balance and began to fall—straight backward.

In that instant, all I could think was, *"Lord, help me."*

I truly believed it was the end. But something unexpected happened.

It felt as if I were caught mid-air by something soft—like cotton batting—and gently placed back on my feet. A wave of warmth surrounded me, like a heater blowing directly on my body. And just like that, the fear disappeared.

I didn't catch myself. I didn't brace for impact. Something—or someone—intervened.

I like to believe my Guardian Angel was working overtime that day. And for that, I am deeply grateful.

"God goes with me wherever I go."

— A Course in Miracles

33

Uncertainty of a New Life

At the beginning of my pregnancy, I experienced some early complications. I was about three months along when I began having stomach pains. The physician reassured me it was nothing serious, but I couldn't shake the concern.

When I was about five and a half months pregnant, I felt the baby move for the first time. That moment filled me with joy and a deep, overwhelming sense of love.

Not long after, while visiting a friend, I tripped over a hole in her gravel driveway after a heavy rain and fell hard, right onto my stomach.

That night, labor pains began. My husband rushed me to the hospital, and I was admitted immediately.

The next morning, I woke up to a horrific smell in the room—a scent I can only describe as death. My family doctor examined me and quietly moved me to another room. When my husband joined me, I saw the tears in his eyes. That's when I knew something was wrong.

He gently told me the doctors believed we would lose the baby that day.

I was only 25, and while I heard the words, I couldn't fully comprehend what they meant.

The weeks that followed were filled with uncertainty. I was in and out of the hospital. I never felt the baby move again, and the doctors could not detect a heartbeat.

Still, somehow, I carried the pregnancy to full term. Labor lasted for three long days.

Then, my beautiful baby boy was born—alive and crying, with big brown eyes and weighing eight and a half pounds.

From the moment we brought him home, he slept peacefully through the night.

Through every frightening moment, I felt God's presence. He guided me, held me, and gave me strength I didn't know I had.

Even when all signs pointed to loss, God stayed with me—reminding me that I was never alone.

"For I know the plans I have for you," declares the Lord, "plans to prosper you and not to harm you, plans to give you hope and a future."

— Jeremiah 29:11

34

Healing the Size of a Glacier

About a year ago, my family and I took a trip to Anchorage, Alaska. One of the highlights was a breathtaking helicopter ride that would land on a glacier. But the night before this exciting adventure, I was overwhelmed by severe vertigo that left me unable to sleep.

A few months earlier, I had learned some self-care techniques from my acupuncturist, but that night, nothing seemed to help. I was filled with doubt.

How could I possibly get on a helicopter like this?

The next morning, as we made the hour-long drive to the helipad, I curled up in the back seat, silently praying for relief. I felt helpless, and honestly, a little hopeless.

But then—I looked up.

Through the windshield, I saw a mountain standing tall in the distance, bathed in light. In that moment, something shifted. It felt like the seas had parted. I was calmed. I was safe.

By the time I boarded the helicopter, I felt ready. As we lifted into the sky and soared over Alaska's breathtaking landscape, I gazed down at the stunning, sky-blue glaciers rising from the water below.

Sitting up front beside the pilot, I felt like I had discovered heaven on Earth. Peace washed over me in a way I had never known.

When we landed and stepped out onto the glacier, I was walking on a masterpiece—ancient, brilliant, and full of grace.

I hadn't just witnessed the glacier's majesty. I had experienced a healing the size of one.

"He makes me lie down in green pastures, he leads me beside quiet waters, he restores my soul."

— Psalm 23:2–3

35

Love and Grace Beyond Understanding

In November 2016, my father was turning seventy, so I decided to take my sixteen-year-old daughter to visit him. She had just received her Canadian passport, and we were excited to spend a special week together in my home country.

When we arrived at the airport to return to Canada, we were stopped. Border authorities informed us that, because my daughter had been born in this country, she would need her father's written permission to leave—until she turned eighteen. Her father, my ex-husband, still lived nearby. When I hadn't spoken to him in years. I was too proud to ask for his help.

Since it was Saturday and the courts were closed, we couldn't get the necessary paperwork. We missed our flight and had to find a hotel in Sofia for several extra nights.

During that time, my daughter became very ill. By Monday, I had no choice but to reach out to her father. I asked him to come and sign the needed papers so we could go home. He agreed.

We met at a coffee shop. My daughter, though still quite unwell, came along briefly. When her father saw her, his face softened with emotion. He brought old books for her—including *The Little Prince*, which she loved.

When it came time to say goodbye, he gently touched my shoulder and looked into my eyes with a love so deep and tender, I was stunned. There was no bitterness in his gaze—only warmth. Only grace.

In that moment, I felt something beyond human love. I believe I was experiencing a glimpse of God's love flowing through him—for me, for our daughter, for the life we had once shared.

We never saw him again. He passed away just a few years later. But that gaze—the look in his eyes—still lives in my memory. Sometimes I wonder if the entire experience, even the missed flight, was God's way of giving my daughter a final moment with her father... and giving me one last reminder of the power of love to soften even the hardest places in our hearts.

It was a gift I didn't understand at the time; now I do.

"Be kind and compassionate to one another, forgiving each other, just as in Christ God forgave you."

— Ephesians 4:32

36

The Story of Brett: Against All Odds

It was Labor Day weekend when my son Brett, just 15 years old, left with our church youth group for a retreat in East Texas. On Friday evening, my husband and I received a devastating call—there had been a car accident. Brett had hit his head and was being Careflighted to an East Texas trauma center.

By divine grace, his sister worked at that very hospital. She helped care for and advocate for him, a powerful sign to me that God was with us in the midst of the tragedy.

As we drove to the hospital, we were told Brett was in the ICU, in a medically induced coma, and receiving IV morphine. We gave verbal consent for doctors to drill holes in his skull to relieve the pressure, though they warned us he likely wouldn't survive. We were in shock—grappling with fear, grief, and disbelief.

I reached out to everyone I could think of—friends, family, church members—asking for urgent prayers.

When we arrived, we met the truck driver who had witnessed the accident and whose quick actions helped save Brett's life. He explained that the woman driving the other car had lost control and collided with the van carrying the kids; she did not survive. The truck driver pulled out Brett's injured friends and then went back to his truck for tools to free Brett. When he finally reached him, Brett wasn't breathing and had no pulse. Then, the driver saw him try to vomit and quickly rolled him to his side—just in time.

By a miracle, Brett survived the surgery. A pastor came to the hospital and gently said, "From this day forward, your lives have changed forever."

Brett was placed on a ventilator and connected to countless tubes. They wouldn't let me see him at first, fearing that my emotional state might elevate his brain pressure further. When I was finally allowed into his room, my heart broke all over again.

He was later transferred to a rehabilitation center, where he remained in a coma for almost nine months. His total rehab stay lasted eighteen months. He had a tracheostomy and a feeding tube. I trained with therapists so I could bring him home. Brett was a teenager—and I was determined he would not be placed in a nursing home.

Today, Brett is a quadriplegic and unable to speak. He is completely dependent on others, but he can still smile—and follow movement with his eyes.

For the past 40 years, I've cared for him, while also working in healthcare for 34 years. This journey has taught me more than I could ever describe. I understand the pain, fear, and love that families carry. My heart overflows with compassion for those I serve.

Through Brett's life, I have come to know grace—and the quiet honor of being a blessing to others.

"My grace is sufficient for you, for my power is made perfect in weakness."

— 2 Corinthians 12:9

37

Prayer Room on a Soup Kitchen Bus

For several months, I've volunteered at a mobile soup kitchen that serves areas where unhoused people gather. The organization is Christian-based but not overly preachy; their mission focuses on helping people find housing, not just handing out soup. In fact, three individuals found a place to live this week thanks to their efforts.

On the bus, there's a section called the "prayer room," where we distribute blankets, jackets, gloves, socks, hygiene kits, and other necessities—and offer prayer for those who want it. Yesterday, several volunteers weren't able to come, so I was asked to stay on the bus and serve in that space.

Normally, I'm outside mingling—serving soup, listening to stories, just trying to be a loving presence. But the prayer room is small—only one person can come in at a time. After they choose what they need, I ask if they'd like prayer. Not one person turned me down.

Wearing masks, we looked into each other's eyes—soul to soul. They shared pieces of their lives, and I listened.

One young man, after I prayed for him and reminded him he is a child of God, had tears in his eyes. He hugged me, and I held him until he was ready to let go.

One woman told me she sees evil spirits at night. After we prayed together, she said she felt a warm sensation surrounding her—one that didn't grow cold.

Another woman spoke of living in a tent with her husband and her fear about the coming snowstorm. I offered her a couple of extra blankets. She hesitated—she didn't want to seem greedy—but then asked me to pray for a place to stay.

I went that day hoping to make a difference.

By the time I left, I knew—they had made a difference in me.

"The best way to find yourself is to lose yourself in the service of others."

— Mahatma Gandhi

38

Kindness Speaks Louder

In a rural Texas town, I was attending an annual workshop taught by my painting mentor. The only place open for breakfast was a local barbecue joint that also served coffee. It doubled as the gathering spot for ranchers and cowboys—men who sipped their coffee while solving the world's problems using colorful language.

The walls were covered with signs—pro-gun rights, anti-gay slogans, climate change denial, and declarations that Trump had won the election. The atmosphere was thick. As I walked in, I whispered to myself, "God be with me, I'm going in."

I felt completely out of place, but I ordered breakfast and quietly scrolled through my phone, trying to tune out the conversations swirling around me. After I finished eating, I did what I always do: I wrote a small thank-you note to the staff, appreciating them for their kindness and for simply showing up to feed others that day. On my way out, I handed the note to the rough-looking cowboy who owned the place.

As I was getting into my car, he came out with tears in his eyes. "This is the nicest thing that's happened to me in a long time," he said, before wrapping me in a big hug. "The world needs more people like you." Tears welled up in my eyes too.

When I returned for breakfast the next morning, my note was taped beside the coffee pot for all to see.

That moment stayed with me. A quiet act of kindness had built a bridge between two people from very different walks of life. I truly believe God was with us both.

"Wherever there is a human being, there is an opportunity for kindness."

— Seneca

39

Dragged to Safety; Carried by Grace

On March 15, 1999, my daughter Janet's life—and mine—changed forever. She was only a teenager, traveling with her best friend Nancy, Nancy's younger sister Emily, and their father Rick. They had flown from Texas to Austin, then set out in a rental car for Montana. I can't recall exactly why they were going, but I will never forget the trip—or its aftermath.

Outside of Missoula, Montana, after driving nonstop with no sleep, Rick likely nodded off at the wheel. The car veered off the road and rolled one and a half times. No one was wearing seatbelts. Janet had been leaning against the back door. When the car stopped rolling, Rick and Janet were no longer inside.

Nancy later told me that when she opened her eyes, she couldn't see her dad or Janet. Her little sister Emily was crying in the front seat, still in place. Nancy climbed out and found her dad lying motionless several feet away. Then she saw Janet, unconscious in the middle of the highway. Nancy, small and seemingly fragile, somehow found the strength to drag Janet out of the road.

That's where I believe divine intervention stepped in.

Moments after Nancy got Janet to safety, a semi truck passed by—the very driver who called in the accident. One more second, and things might have ended very differently.

Janet was airlifted to a nearby hospital with five pelvic fractures and a traumatic brain injury. When I got the call, I was shattered. I couldn't think clearly, so I phoned my brother, who booked my flight. I cried nonstop. The flight attendants were so kind, they moved me to first class to keep an eye on me. Airport staff walked me to my connecting flight. I was overwhelmed by their compassion.

When I arrived, Janet was in a medically induced coma. At first, she didn't recognize me. When she could finally speak, she asked, "Who are you?" I told her, "I'm your mom." She blinked and replied, "You mean I have two moms?" I didn't know who she thought the other one was, but I clung to hope.

Because of her injuries, Janet was placed in a hospital bed that restricted movement. She didn't understand why she couldn't get up. I was terrified she would fall and hurt herself more. I didn't trust the nurses to watch her closely—not because they didn't care, but because they were stretched so thin. So I stayed, refusing to leave her side, until sleep deprivation finally took its toll. I had nowhere to rest, so I curled up under a desk in an empty office. Someone found me there and eventually helped me to a bed. That moment—utterly exhausted, broken, and scared—still haunts me.

Dan, Janet's dad and my ex-husband, was there the whole way. I don't want to leave him out. He flew with us, stayed nearby, and visited often. I stayed constantly, and he found comfort knowing I was there when he returned to the hotel. We were both on the flight that transferred Janet to a children's hospital back in Texas. She had to be intubated for the flight, but thankfully, it was smooth.

At the next hospital, she received excellent care. By then, she was aware and could understand what was happening. She improved enough to transfer to a rehabilitation center, where she learned to walk again. I wish I could remember the name of the rehab facility—but so much of that time is a blur.

What stands out most isn't the hospitals or the procedures—it's the kindness.

I was a high school art teacher and had to take time off to be with Janet. My coworkers donated their sick leave and even sent money to help. People I barely knew stepped in to support us. Our church raised funds and offered help before we could even ask. Janet's friends welcomed her back with open arms.

Today, Janet lives in the country with her husband. She raises chickens, ducks, honeybees—and three wonderful children. She sometimes substitutes at the local elementary school and is still the gifted artist she's always been. She takes good care of her family, and by all accounts, has made a full recovery.

When I look back, I don't just see trauma—I see overwhelming kindness. The kindness of strangers. The kindness of friends. And the quiet, fierce strength of a girl named Nancy who pulled my daughter from the road that day—strength I know came straight from God.

That's what I remember most: the love, the help, and the unmistakable presence of God in our darkest hour.

That's why I believe.

"Underneath are the everlasting arms."

— Deuteronomy 33:27

40

Vehicle of Love

A few years ago, I felt inspired to cover a small hole near the glove compartment on the passenger side of my car. Though I don't consider myself an artist, I bought a set of crayon paint markers and decided to get creative.

Back in the 1970s, I used to love drawing the word "love" in big, bubbly letters—so I painted it on the glove compartment.

The result surprised me. It felt playful, joyful, and right. I was glad I listened to that quiet nudge of inspiration.

Since then, I've driven thousands of miles between home and Phoenix, transporting people who need to see medical specialists. Every person who's ridden in my car has seen that painted word—love—greeting them as they got in. I've received so many kind comments over the years. Somehow, that one word helped create an atmosphere of warmth and safety.

Lately, I've been reflecting on the journey my car has taken—now with over 300,000 miles. I truly believe that the simple act of painting "love" infused my car with a kind of energy. It's just a vehicle, yes—but it has become so much more.

I often give it a gentle pat and whisper thanks for carrying not just me, but so many others. I know it's just an object, but I feel a quiet force has transformed it into something else.

A vehicle of love.

"Love is the way I walk in gratitude."

— A Course in Miracles

"Let all that you do be done in love."

— 1 Corinthians 16:14

41

Intersection of Fear Turned Into Faith

After a hectic morning of driving people all over Kansas City, I was finally on my way home. I stopped at a traffic light near a construction zone, following the directions from my GPS. It told me to turn left—but as I moved forward, I realized I was going the wrong way.

Two lanes of traffic were turning left on the other side of the overpass, headed directly toward me. I stopped my car in the middle of the intersection. I didn't feel afraid, exactly—just aware that I wasn't where I was supposed to be. It was as if time slowed down.

This intersection is usually busy, but in that moment, there was very little traffic. No horns blared. No angry drivers. The cars simply maneuvered around me and continued on. It took less than a minute for the road to clear so I could turn around and head in the right direction.

But that minute felt full of something more.

I sensed a calming, protective energy around me—as though angels were guiding not just me, but the other drivers too. What could have been a dangerous accident became instead a moment of quiet correction, wrapped in grace. I truly believe my angels were there, helping me find my way safely home.

"I am with you and will watch over you wherever you go."

— Genesis 28:15

42

Miracles Everyday

Many times, I find myself oblivious to the blessings in my life, forgetting that I truly live a charmed existence. I often focus more on what goes wrong than on what goes right.

A few days before Christmas, we took my beloved Australian Shepherd, Gracie, to the vet for lab work. This past fall, we said goodbye unexpectedly to two of our fur babies just weeks apart. The lab results for Gracie indicated that her levels for Cushing's Disease kept climbing. In September, we were told that if her levels went up any higher, she would need treatment. I was beginning to prepare myself for the beginning of the end. When I got the call from the vet with the results, he said the tests were normal— not even in the "high normal" range. He also mentioned that once this lab value starts to climb, it is rare for it to return to normal.

That afternoon, I thought I wouldn't be able to see my youngest son and his family, as he is the director of facility management at a large Christian church. However, he called and wanted to get together on Christmas Eve because he had his church duties covered. Even though we live about 15 minutes apart, we rarely see each other. The time we spent together was fun and filled with love.

On Monday, our refrigerator broke down. I told my husband how wonderful it was that it waited until after Christmas to fail. We were able to pick one out and have it delivered the next day. I felt very blessed, especially knowing that a friend in another state had to wait over five weeks for her new one and almost paid twice for a smaller model.

Then, yesterday, my granddaughter was at her boyfriend's house. As she was getting ready to leave, she thought, "Just five more minutes." Suddenly, they heard a loud crash. They ran outside to find her car halfway down the street. A speeding driver had run into her car, likely totaling both vehicles. We are so grateful she wasn't inside it.

We are always living in a season of miracles, but we don't always realize it. Miracles can be both big and small and everything in between. I truly feel that we live a "charmed life." I know miracles of all kinds surround us every day.

"There is no order of difficulty in miracles. One is not 'harder' or 'bigger' than another."

— A Course in Miracles

43

Egyptian Awakening!

My journey into spirituality began in my early teens, fueled by a curiosity about what transpired in a spiritualist church. As I grew older, I started attending these churches, participating in circles, learning meditation, becoming a healer, and immersing myself in various workshops. However, as my career took off and life became busier, I unfortunately sidelined my spiritual interests for several years.

In 2011, I had a fortuitous encounter with a wonderful woman who was organizing a spiritual group trip to Egypt for the special date of 11/11. Despite knowing little about my life or beliefs, she invited me to join the group. Initially, I declined, but after careful consideration, I eventually decided to go. It turned out to be the most magical experience of my life!

Months before this trip, a medium had told me that I was lagging in my spiritual development and needed to get my life in order. I believe that the invitation to Egypt was a divine nudge from spirit to help me realign my path.

Throughout the journey, I experienced many extraordinary moments that challenged my belief system in profound ways. Here are a few that still resonate with me fourteen years later:

At the beginning of my Egyptian adventure, whilst wandering through a particular temple, an Egyptian caretaker pulled me aside and took me into a small, dimly lit room adorned with hieroglyphics. He raised my arm and placed my hand on a specific area of the wall, holding it there for several minutes. Though I was unsure of his intentions, I instinctively trusted him and went along with it. Soon after, I began to feel unwell, as he had awakened my kundalini energies. While this can be a risky process, I felt it was part of a plan to connect me with higher energies and redirect my spiritual journey.

A few days later, while exploring the Valley of the Kings, I was struck by a profound sense of familiarity. I felt as though I had once painted the hieroglyphics on the walls. Interestingly, the heel of my hand began to ache, which prompted a medium standing behind me to share insights about my past life, claiming that my body was buried in the exact chamber we were standing in. She explained that the workers there were never allowed to leave due to their knowledge of sacred secrets.

The most extraordinary experience, however, occurred during a meditation session outside the entrance to a temple. We sat upon a wall, with a narrow gravel path running parallel behind us—an area that didn't serve a purpose for foot traffic. Whilst we meditated, I heard loud footsteps crunching on the gravel, which annoyed me, as I felt it was disrespectful for someone to walk so close during our meditation. When I mentioned this to the group leader, she laughed and said, "Darling, there was nobody there; those were Angels walking behind us!"

At that moment, I didn't fully believe her, but there was no one in sight. Feeling an unexplainable urge, I looked up at the sky and noticed a cloud shaped like a large heart. Within the middle of that heart, I saw an exquisite staircase formed by the clouds. This surreal image was hard for me to dismiss, and although I resisted fully accepting it, years later, I learned that witnessing such a phenomenon indeed signifies the presence of Angels. It felt like spirit was gently urging me to embrace my extraordinary experiences.

Looking back, I am filled with awe at how destiny guided my journey to Egypt with that specific spiritual group to reignite my awakening. I have come to appreciate the remarkable patience that spirit has shown me over the years, and I now wonder how I ever doubted their guidance!

"Do not forget to show hospitality to strangers, for by so doing some have entertained angels without knowing it."

— Hebrews 13:2

44

The Weight of Unspoken Words

Art has always been a passion of mine, with watercolor painting holding a special place in my heart. I enjoy painting almost anything, but there's something especially meaningful about capturing the spirit of animals. When someone loses a beloved pet, I often paint a memorial portrait as a gesture of comfort and remembrance.

When my friend's dog passed away, she asked me to paint a full-body portrait instead of my usual headshot. I spent several days working on it, refining every detail and seeking honest feedback from my toughest critics—my husband and my mentor. Their insights helped me make adjustments until I felt confident that the portrait was ready.

Yet when I presented it to her, I could tell it didn't meet her expectations. She pointed out what she saw as flaws: the eyes weren't quite right, the coat was too short, and the color seemed off. In the end, she decided to use a photograph instead. Our communication abruptly stopped. I was left feeling hurt and confused.

The experience weighed on me, so I spoke with my spiritual advisor. He encouraged me to reach out and explain that I had invested significant time and materials—and that a partial reimbursement might be appropriate. I considered it, but ultimately couldn't bring myself to say the words.

About a year later, we crossed paths and exchanged polite nods. The tension was still there. Another year passed, and we met again at a conference. Though we spoke briefly, the discomfort between us remained unspoken. I've always believed in the value of clarity. If two people can't resolve a misunderstanding, how can we expect entire nations to find peace?

With my heart pounding, I approached her and asked if we could talk. She agreed. We stepped aside to a quiet space, and I shared how the experience had affected me—the weight of silence, the sadness of a fractured connection. She listened quietly, her expression softening as I spoke. Then she embraced me, and we both cried.

That moment of vulnerability opened a path to healing. We mended the rift and found a deeper understanding of one another. It reminded me that sometimes, the hardest conversations are the ones that free us—and that connection, when restored, is grace.

"To forgive is to set a prisoner free and discover that the prisoner was you."

— Lewis B. Smedes

45

In the Wake of Loss: Pain Becomes Purpose

The worst, most painful experience of my life ultimately brought about numerous miracles and moments of joy.

As I pulled into my driveway, I noticed something unusual: my dog, Charlie Jo, was not standing at the door to greet me. My husband of 37 years had ridden his bike to work that day, and with the rain pouring down, I assumed he might be calling for a ride home. I rushed inside to answer the phone, my heart racing.

"Hello, this is such-and-such hospital," the voice said. "Dr. So-and-so is calling to inform you that your husband is bleeding from his head and is unresponsive. Are you going to come here?"   In that moment, my world changed forever. I was alone at home with my loyal, beautiful canine companion, and I could feel shock washing over me. My husband had been struck by a distracted driver while riding his bicycle home from work—it was July 11th, 2011.

In the aftermath, Sedona, AZ, became my sanctuary for healing, even more so than before. During this time, I felt a spiritual connection urging me to create a film that would touch people's hearts and help them heal from grief while aiding my own recovery. I realized that, since I would constantly be grappling with my husband's death, expressing my story creatively could be a path to healing.

Thus, "GHOSTBIKE" was born and premiered at the Sedona Film Festival in 2014. I traveled to numerous film festivals across the country, sharing my healing journey and spreading the vital message to avoid distracted driving. It was miraculous to meet and connect with many individuals who had similar stories or were moved by mine.

Spirit reached out to me once more, suggesting that I write a book. Initially, I was overwhelmed. How could I possibly do that? But while in Sedona, I discovered a writing workshop and attended three sessions before finally committing to my writing journey. This led to the publication of "Remember His Name" in 2017, which offers a deeper exploration of my grief and healing process. Its central message encourages people to say the names of those who have passed away, recognizing the importance of remembrance for the loved ones left behind.

I feel incredibly blessed to have been guided to share these crucial messages. What began as a deeply painful tragedy has transformed into a story of triumph and joy.

"Grief is in two parts. The first is loss. The second is the remaking of life."

— Anne Roiphe

46

Awakening in the Dark to Find the Light

My Dark Night began in 2019, when I was only sixteen and had little understanding of spirituality. I felt trapped in a personal hell, unconsciously suppressing waves of trauma, fear, and wounds I couldn't name—some that felt older than this lifetime. I was numb, haunted, and disconnected—from myself, from God, and from meaning.

Then in 2022, at age nineteen, I came across a video by a spiritual teacher whose words struck me to the core. Though I had some awareness of spiritual ideas, I still lacked a conscious connection to God. When I heard him say, *"I know you who are watching do not believe; you do not realize spirituality includes God, not just religion,"* it felt like lightning. It wasn't just a coincidence—it was my first true epiphany in this lifetime.

Part of me resisted. My ego was suspicious. But another part—the deeper, truer part—felt seen. For the first time, I sensed that I had been lost, and now I was beginning to be found. Though I've never met this teacher in person, my soul began to awaken. I felt the quiet, steady presence of the Divine Mother begin to guide me.

Before this moment, I had been a seeker. I'd studied teachings, but I hadn't yet opened my heart. This was different. This was a direct experience of God. Since then, I have chosen the Spirit of God as my guide, healer, comforter—even as a divine parent. I now understand the Divine Mother knows each of us better than we know ourselves.

I strive to live with humility and childlike wonder, surrendering my thoughts and ego each day for healing and transformation. Astrology suggests my Dark Night may continue for a decade. To the ego it feels daunting—but in God's Reality, time is an illusion, and grace allows us to choose again in any moment.

Through this journey, I've gained deep insight, meaningful relationships, connection with my soul family, and the tools to face life's shadows with trust. Old wounds still resurface—greater light often reveals greater shadow—but now I know how to walk through it with God.

I see through the illusions now: the programming, the false beliefs, the pain that once defined me. We are all Holy Children of God, gently being stripped of what no longer serves us, at a pace we can handle. The truth is—we never left the Light. And I hope to help others remember that, too.

"In a spiritual encounter, all relationships are seen as mirrors of the self, while the heart remains open to freely express and receive love without possessiveness."

— Michael Mirdad

47

Messages of God's Love

I am deeply grateful for God answering my unspoken prayers from long ago. These weren't traditional prayers, but rather subconscious pleas for help. I remember a day in class when I was daydreaming, and my teacher noticed and asked if I was okay, bringing everyone's attention to me. I brushed it off at the time, but now I recognize that it was God speaking through her, allowing her to see me with divine insight, or in other words, with God's eyes.

Recently, I had a stressful day at work and found myself desperately asking for a sign. I was feeling anxious. When I returned home, I discovered that my dad had given me a canvas. It was beautifully adorned with the word "LOVE," along with roses and butterflies. I hung it on the wall opposite my bed, and each day when I see it, I know it carries a message from God.

Reflecting on the journey of learning about Jesus has been significant. Growing up, I had heard little about Him, often only receiving judgmental opinions instead. But then, I had a dream where Jesus visited me. In the dream, I was in a busy field, distracted by my phone. When I looked up, I saw Him parting the clouds and stepping forward, visible only to me. We shared a moment of reverence, and then He waved goodbye. The experience felt simple yet profound, especially as many UFOs were tumultuously swirling in the sky, which vanished upon His arrival. He encouraged me by saying, "Good job, keep going," and so I shall, with His guidance.

I feel incredibly blessed and grateful for all the signs, confirmations, and guidance I've received. Above all, I am thankful for God's presence and the Divine Love that surrounds me.

"Before they call I will answer; while they are still speaking I will hear."

— Isaiah 65:24

48

Kindness at the Curb

About 20 years ago, I lived in a little 2-bedroom bungalow in a historical district that I adored. However, there was tension with the couple living across the street; one of the women made it clear that she hated cats. One day, she trapped my cat and sent it to the animal shelter, which created further friction between us. Yet, I was determined not to hate her and prayed for her and that I could forgive her.

At that time, I was unaware of how severely ill I was. I kept developing pneumonia and felt exhausted constantly. I also started seeing geometric shapes in the vision of one of my eyes. When I finally visited an ophthalmologist, he referred me to an infectious disease doctor. After running some tests, the doctor revealed that I was very sick—not only was I HIV positive, but I was also in full-blown AIDS. I left with a handful of prescriptions that made me feel weaker and even more ill.

One afternoon, the day before trash day, I was taking my trash bin to the curb when I lost control of it. The bin tipped over, spilling its contents everywhere. I tried to pick it up but found I didn't have the strength. Feeling defeated, I sat on the curb and cried as I tried to gather my strength.

The neighbor who had previously sent my cat to the pound came out, picked up the trash bin, and began gathering the scattered trash. I told her not to touch it, tears streaming down my face, and pleaded with her not to help. She responded gently, asking what was wrong. I shared with her that I had just been diagnosed with AIDS. She reassured me, saying, "Well, I can't get it from picking up trash." Later that day, she returned with dinner and offered her and her partner's assistance if I ever needed anything. Before leaving, she said, "You know, this isn't a death sentence. Take your meds, and this will be something you live with, not something you die from."

Several years later, that same neighbor returned with two flea-bitten kittens that were just barely 4 weeks old. Their mother had been hit and killed by a car, and she asked if I could take care of them. She smiled and assured me I wouldn't have to worry about her trapping them.

This taught me that even when someone does an unkind act, that doesn't mean they lack compassion, and kindness can come through even in the darkest of times.

Love your enemies, do good to those who hate you."

— Luke 6:27

49

My Journey to God

A miracle in my life began when I discovered a spiritual teacher whose guidance helped me build a stronger faith in God than I had ever known. My journey toward that connection started through a series of seemingly unrelated steps.

At the time, I was involved with the Unity Church community and had originally found my way there through Al-Anon, a support group for the friends and families of alcoholics. A close friend from my local community was preparing to move out of state and invited me to join her on a trip to Sedona, Arizona. Curious, I searched online to see if a Unity Church existed there—and to my surprise, it did.

That simple search opened the door to something much larger. I learned the Sedona church streamed its services online, so I began tuning in and even joined a Friday night group focused on self-help topics. By the time I visited the church in person, I already felt a connection.

When I walked in, rock music filled the space—specifically "The Age of Aquarius." I remember laughing and thinking, *I've come home to my people!* I danced around the room joyfully, finally meeting in person someone I'd interacted with online. I had hoped it might lead to a relationship, but quickly discovered he was married. Embarrassed, I laughed it off—especially after the spiritual teacher joked, "What is this, Hookups.com?" His humor, though brash, helped ease my discomfort and opened my heart. I've always believed that laughter heals pain.

Meeting the community in person and shedding my usual stoic exterior was a turning point. When they asked if any visitors were present, I was given a small bracelet—a simple, welcoming gesture that meant so much. That trip, the visit to the Grand Canyon, and connecting with this teacher marked the beginning of a deep and lasting relationship with God and the Holy Spirit.

It wasn't one moment, but a series of them, woven together in love and laughter. A journey of small miracles—leading me home.

"You didn't come here to find God. You came here to remember you never left."

— Michael Mirdad

50

Miracles Amidst the Struggles

After completing a bachelor's degree in Social Work and Abnormal Psychology in Illinois, I moved to Washington, hoping to find a job. I initially pursued a position as a Tobacco Cessation Counselor, but I struggled with the scripted calls and ultimately turned it down. Instead, I took on a paper route while also working as an adult daycare counselor at a mental health facility. As financial challenges mounted and my father suggested I consider a shelter, I realized that obtaining a Master's degree was crucial for securing better pay for myself and my 16-year-old daughter. With little to no child support from my ex, I was increasingly worried about my mounting credit card debt and the growing pile of bills. Working as a Paraeducator for the school district proved to be a pivotal moment. I came across a flyer for Self-Help Housing and, despite my low hopes, was thrilled to qualify; it felt like a miracle. This opportunity enabled me to strive for a more independent life. While balancing my part-time work with the school district, I also took a weekend job as a reception clerk at a Naval Hospital ER, which helped ease my financial struggles. A year later, I received a federal job offer from the Veterans Health Administration. To prepare, I completed a year-long Health Administration course. Although this new position required a two-hour commute to Seattle, the higher salary and pension benefits felt like another miracle in my journey.

While we were constructing my house—a project where my neighbors and I committed to working every Saturday—I had a serious accident. I fell 20 feet from the second floor onto a pile of siding and a concrete driveway below. The house was in the framing phase, and I was reinforcing nails along the edge. As I was hammering them in, I lost my balance and fell. My last conscious thought was a panicked, "Oh no! What am I going to do?" Drawing on my military training, I instinctively decided to tuck and roll. Although I wasn't a particularly religious person, I believed in God and felt that He sent angels to guide my fall. While I didn't think this was my last moment, realistically, the outcome could have been fatal. A mere inch in any direction could have resulted in a broken neck or potentially life-altering injuries. Thankfully, there was a nurse among our crew who was able to help me. I found myself in and out of consciousness, struggling to get up and walk it off.

Even though I'm not particularly religious, I believe in God. I can't ignore the positive turns my life has taken and the seemingly miraculous events unfolding around me.

"He will give his angels charge over you, to guard you in all your ways."

— Psalm 91:11

51

Will Never Let Me Go

Ever since I first heard about the Camino de Santiago, I felt drawn to it. I dreamed of walking the pilgrimage in Spain with my children, who were teenagers at the time and open to the idea. But their mother didn't approve of taking them out of the country, though she said maybe the following year. I was disappointed—but looking back, I see the grace. That year, our youngest had emergency surgery for appendicitis. The next year, the world shut down from COVID-19.

My wife and I had been best friends since grade school. We married during college, built a life together, and raised our children with love. But during those years, I went through a spiritual and emotional crisis. I realized that although I loved her deeply, I could no longer live the lie—I was gay. We agreed to separate and co-parent our kids with care and respect.

Years passed. The kids became adults and didn't have three months to take a "long hike" with their dad. Still, the longing to walk the Camino never left me.

One morning, I went to a local café for breakfast. A priest was waiting to be seated and invited me to share his table. I hesitated—I believe in God, but I'm not Catholic or even very religious. Still, I said yes.

After we ordered, he looked at me gently and said, "Mijo, you have sad eyes."

Something in me opened, and I found myself telling him everything. About marrying my best friend. About coming out. About hurting someone I loved. About the Camino. He listened without judgment. Then he asked, "What's stopping you from walking it now?"

I lowered my voice and said, "I'm afraid I won't find God."

The priest reached across the table and said, "Oh, Mijo… God has already found you—and He will never let you go."

When we parted, he gave me his card and told me his door was always open.

Not long after, I called my wife and invited her to dinner. I told her I still wanted to walk the Camino—and asked if she'd go with me. She said yes. We trained, planned, and set out together.

It was the most physically demanding thing I've ever done. Our backpacks grew heavier by the hour. Even in good shoes, our feet blistered. But we walked—together. We talked, we laughed, we cried. At the churches along the way, we laid down our burdens and found rest for our bodies and souls. We met other pilgrims and shared stories, sorrow, and hope.

Somewhere along that winding road, my priorities shifted. I saw that my life's circumstances hadn't changed—but my heart had. My responses, my awareness, my peace had changed. This journey was more than a walk—it was a sacred transformation.

About two weeks in, we paused to watch the most breathtaking sunrise I have ever seen. In that still moment, I remembered the priest's words.

God had found me. And I knew… He would never let me go.

"In their hearts humans plan their course, but the Lord establishes their steps."

— Proverbs 16:9

52

My Path to Peace

Throughout my life, I have been deeply inquisitive. I question everything, 'What is our purpose in life?' 'Why does the world work the way it does?' 'Is Jesus Christ real?' 'Is there truly a higher power?'

As a teenager, I wrestled with these questions daily. My mind was restless, searching for meaning, yet I felt mentally lost. In high school, I identified as agnostic—not because I rejected faith, but because I couldn't reconcile the idea of a higher power with my understanding of the world. I yearned for clarity, for a sign that something greater existed.

Meanwhile, my close friends each experienced moments of personal revelation—moments that made them certain of Jesus' reality. I watched them find peace and certainty, and I couldn't help but wonder, 'When would I have my moment?'

My moment of revelation came during the fall semester of my sophomore year in college. I was struggling to find happiness in anything I did, it was a nightmare. I was depressed and overwhelmed with anxiety and uncertainty about my future. I was miserable both physically and mentally. I felt like I was drowning, desperate for something to hold onto.

So I began to pray. They weren't elaborate prayers, just quiet, simple ones asking for protection, asking for a sign. Over time, I began to realize something, not everyone receives a dramatic sign. Everyone's journey is different, and maybe faith doesn't always come with fireworks—it sometimes comes with stillness, with persistence, with surrender.

So that is what I did, I kept praying and began to read the gospel, and the lord began to reveal himself to me in simple ways. I began to find happiness in the little things in life. The beauty of nature, the ability to attend a great university, and the ability to live a healthy life. My life was never truly miserable—I just couldn't see the full picture at the time. Now I realize that everything I went through was part of Jesus' plan for me. He has always been there, even when I couldn't feel it. I came to understand that He suffered on the cross so we wouldn't have to carry the full weight of our pain alone.

I didn't begin to ignore my problems or expect Jesus to fix everything for me. Instead, I brought my worries and stresses to Him in prayer. And through that honest communication, He gave me guidance, clarity, and peace, helping me grow not only in faith but in maturity.

Over the past two-and-a-half years, I've made great strides in my personal and spiritual life. I am deeply grateful to Jesus Christ for walking beside me every step of the way. My journey is far from over, but I now walk forward knowing I am loved by Christ and strengthened by His presence. And that, to me, is the greatest comfort of all.

"You will seek me and find me when you seek me with all your heart."

— Jeremiah 29:13

53

The Gift of Grief

Losing a loved one is painful! No one can disagree with that statement. I lost my husband, Bill, in December of 2023. I want to say that the time since then has been a time of huge spiritual growth that has allowed the extraordinary to be almost ordinary, the feelings of oneness with the divine. Let me explain.

About six months after his death, I bought a puppy to help with the loneliness. She brought me so much more than companionship. I began to notice how curious she was about everything. As I watched her in the yard, noticing, smelling, even tasting every tiny thing she could find, I suddenly became a part of every little or big thing she saw, a feeling of being a part of the whole universe. The experience had a profound effect on me spiritually. It was a warm and beautiful feeling. I wanted more of that serenity. I soon realized that this was a form of meditation or connecting with the divine. I began to read about prayer and meditation. I wanted to keep that feeling of being part of the divine.

What a gift! Yes, I still have moments of sadness, but this time of grief has broadened my awareness of divine presence that may not have happened without this time of loss.

We always have a choice—a miserable time of loss or an opportunity for a wonderful awareness of the divine.

"Death is not extinguishing the light; it is only putting out the lamp because the dawn has come."

— Rabindranath Tagore

54

From Chaos to Tov

This title reflects my transformation from struggle to wholeness. When Yah created the world and called it good, it wasn't good in the human sense of the word—filled with subjective reverence—but rather, it was "tov." Tov encompasses much more than mere goodness; it signifies a deeper alignment with life, fulfilling an intended purpose that often centers around sustaining existence.

Growing up, I lived in chaos. My uncle was a destructive force—an alcoholic, violent, manipulative, and unaccountable. Poverty and falsehood surrounded me, and the lessons I learned could have easily shaped me into someone just like him. Instead, I chose to focus on what I didn't want to contribute to and what I didn't want to become.

Navigating these struggles throughout my 20s led me down a path of rebellion. I misunderstood authority and often rejected any attempts at power that sought to control me or others. For a long time, I viewed my upbringing as a flaw, something to escape. However, by the time I reached my 40s, a sense of clarity emerged. I began to realize that those experiences weren't meant to break me; they were intended to shape me.

In hindsight, I see that I am equipped in ways many others might not be. The struggles I endured have prepared me for challenges that others may not even begin to confront. While this has sometimes bred jealousy and misunderstanding in those around me, I hold onto a transformative truth: what initially seemed like ruin has led me to tov—goodness, completeness, and a profound sense of purpose.

As I reflect on my journey, I encourage others to find their own paths, from chaos to tov. Embrace your struggles, for they hold the potential to lead you toward a more fulfilling and authentic life.

"I am not what happened to me. I am what I choose to become."

— Carl Jung

55

The Hidden Gift in What We Lack

Growing up, soda was a big deal in my family. My aunt and uncle always had it at home, and my cousins consumed it constantly. It wasn't just a drink; it was a symbol of being "in." If you weren't drinking soda, you felt left out of the group.

I didn't get to have soda very often. When I did, I would gulp it down as if trying to make up for all the times I went without it. I didn't savor the experience; I drank with urgency, fearing I wouldn't have another chance anytime soon.

Back then, I thought it was unfair—I wanted what everyone else had. However, as the years went by, my perspective changed. My cousins, who enjoyed soda freely, began to face dental problems. Meanwhile, I managed to avoid the worst of it, despite indulging occasionally.

Looking back on my childhood, now in my 40s, I feel a sense of gratitude. What I considered a limitation turned out to be a gift. Often, we resent what we lack and feel deprived. Yet, sometimes, what seems like deprivation is actually protection—a quiet grace guiding us toward something better. It was a blessing in disguise.

"When we lose one blessing, another is often most unexpectedly given in its place."

— C.S. Lewis

56

Leap of Faith: Trusting the Cape

I was raised in the Methodist church and grew up in a small town. Before my baptism, it was customary to study with the preacher to learn about the basics of the church's teachings. My Mother later revealed to me that he almost refused to baptize me because I asked too many questions and was not satisfied with his answers. I remained involved with the church until I was 15, after which I embarked on my own journey to discover a personal, yet not overly intimate understanding of God.

Along the way, I heard a song that deeply resonated in my life. The song was "The Cape," co-written and sung by Guy Clark in the late 80s. He passed away in 2016. Here's a notable excerpt

"He's one of those who knows that life is just a leap of faith

Spread your arms

And hold your breath

Always trust your cape."

If you look up this song, preferably sung by Guy himself, you'll better understand the circle of faith needed during the challenging and tender moments of life. We all need something or someone to rely on and trust throughout our lives. Some things are absolute treasures that, if you're lucky, you will never outgrow! I've come to realize that I don't need to label my beliefs or follow a single path; instead, I choose to honor and respect the leaps of faith, the light in others, and trust in my own "cape".

"To one who has faith, no explanation is necessary. To one without faith, no explanation is possible."

— Thomas Aquinas

57

The Wisdom of Stars

I've never considered myself a religious person. The few times I attended church, I couldn't understand its appeal. The idea of a God who would send people to hell for not believing in His son seemed like a myth to me. I often questioned why a loving God would sacrifice His son for humanity, and I never could make sense of it all.

However, deep down, I always felt that there was something greater out there, but it wasn't the traditional image of God. My true passion has always been astrology. I loved spending nights gazing at the stars. Over the years, my telescopes became larger, more elaborate, and of course, more expensive. Looking up at the stars filled me with wonder and awe, making me feel both incredibly small and insignificant in the grand scheme of the universe.

My mother often told me of a Serbian proverb: "Be humble, for you are made of earth; be noble, for you are made from the stars of the sky." Many nights, I would fall asleep on the ground, lost in the wonder of the night sky. My mom would sometimes come out to cover me up, and even now, when sleep eludes me, I find comfort in looking up at the stars. It brings me a sense of calm and peace, and I fall asleep to wake up with the morning sun.

It's as if the universe itself is whispering secrets to me, reminding me of my place within it. I have come to realize that my search for meaning doesn't have to be confined to traditional beliefs or dogmas. Someone once told me, "Look to the sky, for that is where your salvation comes from." I don't know who or what created the stars and galaxies, but I believe it is a force of Love and Peace. And while I don't know what it is, I have faith IT knows who I am.

"God writes the Gospel not in the Bible alone, but also on trees, and in the flowers and clouds and stars."

— Martin Luther

58

God's Not Finished With Me

One day in 2020—the best year ever—I came home from work and was sharing a glass of wine with my husband while talking about our days and deciding what to make for dinner. I had just returned from a stressful day as a first-year librarian and an appointment for my allergy shot. Suddenly, a terrible headache hit me—much worse than my usual migraines. I told my husband my head was killing me.

He immediately started problem-solving, wondering if I was reacting to the allergy shot. I told him where my EpiPen was, and he administered it. Then, I began to convulse. He panicked, called 911, explained what was happening, and they sent an ambulance.

I woke up two and a half weeks later in the same hospital I had spent time in years earlier for a different reason. When I asked why I was there, the person in the room rolled their eyes and explained that I had suffered a burst aneurysm—a subarachnoid hemorrhage. My husband had called the ambulance quickly, following a plan we had rehearsed, and doctors had inserted a small stent in my brain to control the bleeding. They assured me I would be fine. Yes, whoever's class I was supposed to be in was covered, and all was fine. Apparently, I had done this many times (much like 50 First Dates). This time, though, I remembered. I stayed awake and conscious and didn't forget. However, those two and a half weeks are still gone.

This could have happened anywhere—while driving, at work alone for hours, or at home by myself. But it happened in front of my husband, who reacted immediately. I believe he's the reason I'm still here today.

My neurologist said if it hadn't been caught so quickly, I wouldn't have survived. My surgeon was impressed that I lost no physical function. My mind took a little longer to catch up, but it functions just like before. There is definitely something—or someone—looking out for me.

"The Lord will watch over your coming and going both now and forevermore."

— Psalm 121:8

59

Promise Beyond Time

The first Christmas season after I became a widow, my children were just 3 and 5 years old. It was the summer before that my husband, Kyle, took a motorcycle out for a ride and was struck by a car that lost control. In an instant, our lives changed forever.

Kyle was an excellent mechanic. He worked for Toyota, and on his days off, he had a side job fixing motorcycles. He often reminded me of a promise he made: that he would always take care of me and the kids. Just three weeks before his accident, he surprised me with a brand new SUV, complete with a three-year maintenance warranty. It didn't make much sense to me because he had always managed to keep our older cars running smoothly.

As an R.N., I had a decent job at a hospital, but the hours were long, working 12-hour shifts, with frequent overtime. One day, on my way home from work, I stopped at Walmart to pick up a few gifts for the girls and some groceries. When I reached the checkout, I realized my wallet was missing. I was baffled, unsure of what had happened to it. The cashier seemed annoyed, but then, a kind man standing behind me stepped forward. He asked the cashier how much my total was, and when she told him it was $158.72, he swiped his card to pay. I tried to get his name and address, promising I would repay him, but he smiled and said there was no need. When I persisted, he told me, "You will have many chances to repay me in the future." I was puzzled and asked, "How?" He replied, "When you are able, pay it forward."

Since that day, I have found multiple opportunities to pay it forward. Whenever someone insists on how they can repay my kindness, I tell them to pay it forward.

I often think about that day in Walmart and wonder if it was Kyle watching over us. Each time I am able to help someone, I feel a connection not only to the stranger who helped me but also to the presence of God and Kyle, knowing they are still caring for us.

"Your father knows what you need before you ask him."

— Matthew 6:8

60

God Balances Things Out

My Dad had hemophilia. He bled easily, so there were many things he could not do. There was a tight-knit group of hemophiliac families that we knew well through our local blood center. Despite his physical limitations, my Dad was such a gifted person! He could draw anything, he played guitar and mandolin and sang, he told great stories and always made us laugh, and although he was not physically able to finish High School, he had studied electronics from an early age and could fix anything electronic! These are just a few of his tremendous skills and talents. My mother, a very astute teacher and librarian, would often discuss how gifted many of the hemophiliacs were. She said, "When God sees an area of lack, he makes up for it somewhere else; God has a way of balancing things out." I grew up hearing this. And now, many years later, I look back at my life and marvel at how true that is. One example is that I met and started dating my now husband the very week my dear Mom had a series of strokes. It was unimaginable to me to be without my Mom. And yet, as she declined and eventually passed, my new beau helped me to get through it by praying with me and sharing his experiences with me. He had previously lost his parents. And instead of trying to "fix it" for me, he just let me cry. The day she died, he cried with me. I cannot put words on how deeply comforting that was! I believe that God placed the perfect person in my life for that time to help me get through it. God has a way of balancing things out. The second example I'll share is that as we planned our wedding, I found out I had breast cancer. The very day we were heading to get his tux and to the venue to meet the owner and staff and the florist, the moment we made our first stop, I got the call! So, as difficult as it was going through the process of appointments, diagnoses, treatment plans, etc., in between, I was planning my dream wedding! Isn't that amazing? So today I am cancer-free, praise God, and I got to marry my sweetheart and have the most beautiful wedding just weeks before surgery! I could go on and on, but as I told my sweet sister, any time I have had a really difficult thing in my life, God has given me something wonderful and perfect to get me through it. My beautiful Mom's Heavenly voice rings in my ear, "God has a way of balancing things out!"

"Out of difficulties grow miracles."

— Jean de La Bruyère

61

Prayers Go On

I never got to meet my husband's parents, as they had passed many years before I met my husband. One thing I have heard over and over from family members is what a faithful and devoted Christian woman his mother was. She served Christ in all she did, from raising her 6 children, to church service, to counseling those in need, to doing whatever she was called to do to bring people to Christ. In fact, when she died, her church built a church in the Dominican Republic in her name! I can't even imagine how many prayers she said for her family, community, and all those in need!

Years later, when my husband and I had been happily married for about two and a half years, we had his brother and his wife over for dinner one night. During some aspect of our dinner conversation, something very touching, my husband and I joined hands on the table. No big deal, it's just what we do. Later, my sister-in-law said, "You know God is always answering our prayers. It is ongoing, there is no end." I had never thought of it like that. Then she said something that I will never forget! She said, "I saw you two holding hands at dinner, and I see how happy you are. And I think, can you imagine how much his Mom prayed for this - for him to be happy, to have someone to love, and to have a happy home? Her prayers are still working!" It makes me cry every time I think of it. Thank you, dear sister -in-law, for such a sweet gift! I will never forget this. God bless you!

"The prayer of a righteous person is powerful and effective."

— James 5:16

62

Adventures in Forgiveness

I was in a tight spot. My cousin Joan, who was also my landlady, had given me a year and a half's notice to move out because she needed the space for her oldest daughter. That time had passed, and I was nowhere nearer to moving out than I was when she'd first told me.

The main problem was that I was a single mom with an 8-year-old son and didn't want to take him away from the cozy nest we'd created.

My cousins and their two daughters lived below us, and they felt like siblings to him. We had looked at other apartments, but they all seemed cold, dreary, and lonely compared to our little haven. I even placed ads hoping to find another single mom to share an apartment with, but no one responded. Fortunately, Joan took pity on us and extended my moving deadline by another five months—until June--to figure things out.

I started to fantasize about traveling as a possible solution. Two months later, I was still feeling stuck, so I talked to a very intuitive friend, Mary. She suggested that my feelings of anger towards my cousin for asking us to move out were holding me back. I needed to forgive her to get the energy flowing and things moving forward. Joan had no idea I was angry at her, so I simply proclaimed out loud in my kitchen, "I forgive you, Joan!" Within the hour, I received a call from a single mom about my ad, and we made plans to look for apartments together.

It immediately became clear that our parenting styles and kids weren't a good match, but I'd made a new friend, and the "energy" continued to flow abundantly and positively.

Plans to spend a school year on the road began to take shape, and everything fell into place effortlessly: free storage for our belongings until we returned, free places to stay for the two and a half months until we left, and then a travel itinerary covering a dozen states and provinces from September to June! Friends, family, and even acquaintances we had never met were eager to help us. It felt like everything aligned perfectly simply because I had let go of my anger and opened my heart to forgiveness.

"Forgiveness is the key to peace and freedom."

— A Course in Miracles

63

The Depths of Peace

When I was about 11 years old in 1966, I was at a church picnic. I was new at swimming, but felt pretty confident that I could keep myself afloat. So I ventured into the deeper end of the pool, where I couldn't touch the bottom, and I was pretty proud of myself as I did the dog paddle back to the more shallow end. I thought I had gotten there, so I took a deep breath as I lowered my feet toward the bottom. Alas, it wasn't yet as shallow as I thought, and I ended up taking a deep breath of pool water, which caused me to pass out.

Suddenly, I was aware of this incredible light all around me, and I let myself be drawn into the sublime peace I felt. It really felt wonderful.

The next thing I knew, I was being dragged out of the pool by the lifeguard, and he was hitting my back. I started coughing and choking up water. I didn't go back into the pool right away. My parents had left before all of this happened, and those who had been asked to watch me missed the whole thing until I was coughing on the side of the pool.

In the long run, someone encouraged me to get back in the water, so I did, but I stayed in the shallow end until it was time to go.

Honestly, to this day, I remember the Light and Peace, and as a result, I have never feared death since.

"Peace, I leave with you; my peace I give you. I do not give to you as the world gives. Do not let your hearts be troubled and do not be afraid."

— John 14:27

64

Connected by Love: Mother's Last Gifts

In the late 90s, my mom was on her deathbed in the hospital. When I called the hospital to see how she was, they transferred me to her room, and she answered the phone. I told her I was surprised, and she went on to tell me about her own near-death experience – the Light, the Peace, and actually being with Jesus. But as she basked in the bliss, she was also able to look down at my dad in the waiting room. He was so distraught about losing her that she knew she had to give up the peace and go back to teach my dad how to accept her transition before she could actually ascend. And she did just that.

A few years later, in 2001, she knew she was done, and once again was admitted to the hospital for what they thought was a minor issue. No one was worried, but circumstances were such that, due to an excess of morphine (which had been administered to ease her pain), it had gotten stuck in her arteries, and when they moved her to see what was going on, it was released with a gush, and it took her life. I actually felt it at the exact moment it happened, even without the phone call.

The next morning, I called anyway to see how she was doing, and the nurse told me she had passed. My dad had been in the business office while all this was happening, and when he got to her room, the nurse told him I was on the phone. He told me about how he had gone to complain about her care, and I gently interrupted him and said, "Dad, she's gone." He didn't believe me at first, but the nurse confirmed it, and he was so distraught. However, I knew she was at peace and back with Jesus, and watching over all of us from the other side.

Side note: I travelled to Florida to be with my dad, and he told me about all of the things she had done in the past few years to prepare him – how to cook meals, how to do chores, even that it was okay if he dated other women. But in the long run, he never dated anyone else, and would often talk to her as though she was still there, which, in some form, I believe she was, ever watching over him. In fact, when his time came, I felt her welcoming him to

"What we have once enjoyed we can never lose. All that we love deeply becomes a part of us."

— Helen Keller

65

Bob's Life and Legacy

I met my husband, Bob, in 1974. Even then, he was dealing with significant pain. His hip issues had started back in junior high, but he still persevered and played varsity football in high school. After intense physical activity, though, the pain would catch up with him. He'd spend a week or more on crutches, recovering.

Years later, after we were married, Bob was diagnosed with ankylosing spondylitis. Both hips had to be replaced. The surgeries were successful, but the doctors warned us they would likely need to be redone in five years.

As it turned out, those replacements lasted much longer—nearly 20 years. By then, we were no longer married, but I still followed his health closely. When the time came for the second round of surgeries, the first—his right hip—went relatively well. But the left didn't go as planned. Bob was confined to a wheelchair for nine months. When doctors finally gave him the go-ahead to try again, they discovered his bone density had deteriorated too much for surgery to be possible.

In 2016, Bob was hospitalized and nearly died. I received the call in the middle of the night from my son. I prayed that Bob would choose to let the doctors revive him so I could see him one last time. He had been intubated—something I knew he never wanted—but when I arrived two hours later, he was still alive.

I stayed nearby with a friend that week so I could be close. Three or four days later, the tubes were removed at Bob's insistence. I sat at his bedside for hours as he napped from the ordeal. That evening, I left for the night. In the early morning, I got the call: Bob was likely transitioning. I rushed to the hospital—just minutes away—but by the time I arrived, he had passed. Still, I sat with him. Though his body lay lifeless, I felt his presence all around me—strong and calm. I stayed for several hours, journaling and communing with his spirit. I still feel him with me. He let me know that it was his time, his choice, and that he is blissfully happy now—free from pain, free from human form.

These near-death and after-death experiences have only deepened my understanding that we are eternal beings. This physical world—what we see and touch—is not the full story. It's an illusion that tries to deny our True Beingness. But who we are at our core—our souls— live on, forever connected.

"There is no death. Death is but a change of mind."

— A Course in Miracles

66

A Second Chance Changes Everything

"Stop! There's a rabbit!" I yelled. Nick's voice overlapped mine. We saw it from the back seat—a little thing darting across the road. We both yelled for the driver to watch out. She swerved gently, giving it a second chance.

But before we could even breathe, a Mustang came out of nowhere, flying past in the wrong lane. The driver yanked the wheel hard—too hard. The truck lurched sideways. Tires screamed. Then came the ditch. I felt the ground disappear beneath us. For a heartbeat, we hung in the air—like the world was holding its breath. Then gravity took us back. The truck hit, bounced, and started to flip, slow and brutal.

I remember the sound of metal twisting and people screaming. The sky is spinning. Weightlessness. Then glass shattered around me, and everything went white. For a moment, I felt like I was nowhere and everywhere. Then—nothing.

The next thing I remember, I was in a hospital bed, hooked up to machines. My back ached like it had been torn open. A nurse told me I'd been thrown from the truck—run over. Literally crushed under a car. There's still a tire mark scar across my back to prove it. One of my vertebrae had flipped upside down. The doctors said it was a miracle I wasn't paralyzed or dead. People don't survive injuries like that. They said the only reason I was alive was because I landed curled up, like I knew what was coming. But I don't remember hitting the ground. I just remember floating—and then the pain.

Nick's arm was torn up so badly, they weren't sure if he'd ever move his fingers again. But after months of recovery, he regained full use. The doctors said I'd be bedridden for three months, but I couldn't accept that. I couldn't just lie there and do nothing. The next day, I got up.

When I got home from the hospital, two rabbits were sitting outside my window. Just sitting there—like they were waiting. They couldn't have been the same ones from the road, but something about it felt like more than a coincidence. It felt like a message. Like maybe I'd been given a second chance, too.

Before the crash, Nick and I were just casual friends—we saw each other now and then, and nothing more. But after what we went through, everything changed. We weren't just friends anymore. We were brothers. We'd been through something together that no one else could understand, and that kind of bond doesn't come from anything else. It's something built on survival, and it sticks with you.

Years later, I still think about it. The world's a little different now—slower, somehow. I don't sweat the small stuff anymore. The things that once had me riled up don't feel as important. I've learned to appreciate the simple things—my apartment, the warmth of my fiancé's smile, the way my dog greets me at the door, and even the quiet moments with my cat. I take life one day at a time now. I stay grounded, grateful—for everything I almost didn't get to keep.

And every time I think about that crash, I remember the bunny we saved—and how, in some strange way, life saved me too. You don't always see second chances coming. But if you're lucky enough to get one, don't waste it.

"Every day is a second chance."

— Unknown

67

Butterflies After 9/11

September 11, 2001, changed many people's lives, including mine. I worked at the World Trade Center. I was always at work by 7:00, if not an hour or more before. On this day, however, I overslept, something I have never done, even as a teen. But this Tuesday morning, it was just after 7:00 when I woke. Hurriedly, I took my shower, grabbed some java, and rushed out the door. If the traffic cooperated, I could get there just after 8:00. From my vehicle, I heard the plane hit the first tower and then the second. Smoke was coming out of both twin towers, and emergency services were en route; every other car was turned away. There was chaos everywhere. I returned home numb and confused. I couldn't comprehend what happened. TV coverage kept showing the planes flying into the building. My neighbor, who worked at the World Trade Center, perished. He had a cat and a dog; I brought them to my home. I was in shock the next few weeks and spent my days petting them as tears soaked their fur. In an instant, I lost my job, my coworkers, my friends, and my neighbor.

My mother wanted me to move back home, but I was not ready. I decided to stay where I was, at least for a while. I didn't have the strength or energy to think about moving when I could barely get out of bed. Another neighbor, who lost his wife, and I started talking. We both confided to each other that we felt guilty about still being alive. We thought about therapy, but all the therapists were booked. Neither one of us was religious, preferring a bar to church. But we decided to attend a Sunday service. I remember the minister saying,

"If you are here, there is a reason. God has something planned for you."

When the service was over, this minister told us his door was open to us. When we left the church that day, several butterflies were flying about. I remember butterflies were special to my secretary. Whenever she saw them, she would say, "Everything is good." It was the day my healing began. I began counseling with the minister and asked him what God had planned for me. He said, "It's to do the next right thing."

"What the caterpillar calls the end of the world, the master calls a butterfly."

— Richard Bach

68

God's Greater Purpose

In the year 2000, I was married and had started a new family in a new city with my 1-year-old son, Justin. I had made some new friends who were also new moms, and we would organize playdates together. One day, I mentioned to my single friend Melissa that I was going to an information session for foster care. I was curious and thought it could be something I would enjoy doing. She asked if she could tag along since she didn't own a vehicle. "Of course," I replied.

During the information session, it occurred to me that my husband would also have to participate, as this would impact the whole family. I immediately thought he might not be interested, so I dropped the idea. However, my friend Melissa signed up that day and never looked back. My husband and I even helped her update her rental home to meet the safety code requirements.

Over the past 25 years, Melissa has fostered many children and adopted two of them along the way. She also serves as a resource for new foster parents. Fostering children is incredibly challenging, and looking back, I know I wouldn't have been able to take on such a mission at that time. Yet, I believe God used me as a vehicle to connect her with the opportunity she was willing and capable of pursuing.

I returned to my hometown in 2003, and a few years ago, Melissa reached out to tell me that I was responsible for her fulfilling career in fostering. That brought joy to my heart, and I felt that God was looking out for those children, knowing exactly who they needed. I am humbled that God saw me as a vehicle—both literally and figuratively—for such a beautiful miracle in the lives of those children and my friend Melissa.

Nothing we do is wasted time or effort; God always has a bigger plan that we may not always see.

And we know that in all things God works for the good of those who love him, who have been called according to his purpose."

— Romans 8:28

69

Signs From God

As a child, I often sensed God's presence. However, as I grew older and busier with life and my own family, that connection seemed to fade into the background. By my 30s, with a young family, I started feeling disenchanted with life and longed for something more. This desire led me to explore self-help and spirituality books.

One particular book encouraged readers to ask God for signs. I was taken aback by how simple this idea was—did it really work? The author suggested using an owl as a sign, so I decided to adopt the same symbol, even though I had no special attachment to owls.

At that time in my career, I faced a decision between two positions at the hospital: one in Transfusion Medicine (TM) and the other in Haematology. Both roles offered the same salary, but one was more challenging and dynamic, while the other was calmer and less stressful. I preferred the work in TM but felt uncertain about my ability to handle the challenges ahead. Conflicted, I asked God for a sign— specifically, to show me an owl if I should take the TM position.

That afternoon, while on a break at the coffee shop, I glanced at the gift shop and saw an owl decoration staring right at me. I immediately dismissed it, thinking it was too easy. After all, gift shops often carry such items. "Sorry, God, but I need another sign," I said to myself.

Later that evening, as I scrolled through Facebook, I spotted an image of an owl in my feed. Again, I dismissed this sign, telling God it was too convenient and asking for a different sign.

The next morning, I returned to work. I had forgotten about my earlier dismissals until my coworker excitedly shared her shift stories. After she finished, she pulled out her phone to show me a birthday cake she had created for an 8-year-old girl. To my astonishment, it was a green fondant owl birthday cake!

At that moment, I was flabbergasted. It hit me how many times I had sought guidance but hadn't thought to simply ask! Now, I realize that we are always supported and guided; we just need to ask without attachment or judgment, and the answers will come.

"Ask, and it will be given to you; seek, and you will find; knock, and the door will be opened to you."

— Matthew 7:7

70

A Journey of Joy and Sorrow

Twenty-seven years ago, I was pregnant with my third child. Although this pregnancy was unplanned, I chose to embrace the new life that was about to enter my world. At that time, my sister and I were also trying to arrange a meeting between our father and his eldest son, whom he had given up for adoption many years before.

Then, just a week before my due date, I received the devastating news that my father had been hit head-on by a drunk driver. He was in a coma and was considered brain-dead. My sister drove from Chicago to Kansas City and then took both of us to the St. Louis area for his funeral.

The afternoon before the service, I went into labor, and I gave birth to my daughter at 3 AM on the day of my father's funeral. It was an incredibly challenging time for me, as I felt immense joy at the birth of my daughter alongside the deep sorrow of my father's passing.

Shortly after, I got a call from my grandmother, who informed me that my father had been born at the same hospital where my daughter was delivered. This brought me a great sense of peace. Miraculously, I was able to attend the funeral service. During that time, I felt the presence of the Divine Mother with me, offering comfort I had never experienced before. Many were astonished that I was even there.

In the weeks that followed, I focused my grief on caring for my newborn baby, which became a very special time of bonding for us. To this day, my daughter and I are very close—I call her my angel, and she has grown to become a nurse, serving many people in need.

That experience brought me closer to God in a way I had never felt before, and for that, I am grateful beyond measure. It taught me that he is always with us, even in moments of loneliness and fear.

You turned my mourning into dancing; you removed my sackcloth and clothed me with joy."

— Psalm 30:11

71

Protected by Angels

In 1995, I welcomed my first grandchild into the world. Holding her for the first time was a profound experience that filled my heart with love, joy, and hope for the future. However, shortly after this beautiful occasion, my life took an unexpected turn. On my way home from work, a semi-truck suddenly veered into my lane, crashing into my car.

In that moment, I instinctively turned to God, thanking Him for the blessings in my life, and asked for the presence of guardian angels. I uttered a simple prayer, asking that if it were my time, to make it quick. Suddenly, a serene calmness enveloped me, as though I was being cradled in safety. I clearly heard a voice urging me to let go of the gas and the steering wheel. Time seemed to stretch indefinitely as the truck struggled to come to a halt, pressing my car against its front.

The driver rushed over, but to my astonishment, I had sustained absolutely no injuries. It was a testament to the protection I felt that day—the presence of my guardian angels was vividly real to me, and I knew without a doubt that they were with me.

In the aftermath of the accident, I found myself reflecting on that day and its significance. It became clear to me that life is fragile and unpredictable, reminding me to cherish every moment with my loved ones.

"If you knew who walks beside you on the way that you have chosen, fear would be impossible."

— A Course in Miracles

72

Heaven is Real

During a pacemaker procedure, something unexpected happened: my heart was punctured. In an instant, I found myself transported to a place of unparalleled beauty. There was Ray, my partner, who had passed away a year earlier. In that moment, we were young again, dressed in our favorite country western outfits, ready to dance like we used to. His smile was radiant, and there were no signs of the cancer that had taken him from me.

As he reached out his hand, I couldn't help but ask about our grandkids, wondering how they were doing. Just as quickly as it had begun, I awoke in the hospital. I learned later that my heart had stopped during the procedure and that I had been shocked back to life three times. It was not a dream; it was real, it was heaven.

This memory is still vivid in my mind; I have no fear of the day when I will be called again. I know that beyond this life, love and joy await, and I can't wait to see Ray once more. Until then, I hold onto the warmth of that moment, cherishing the deep connection we shared and the happiness that transcends even death. I also know that for whatever reason, God is not finished with me. There is more life to live and love to share.

"Nothing... will be able to separate us from the love of God that is in Christ Jesus our Lord."

— Romans 8:38–39

73

Still Standing

What was I going to do?

I was shocked, scared, and confused. I had just received a phone call from my husband—the man I'd been married to for over 30 years. We had raised children together, built businesses, and served our church and community side by side. Now, he was telling me he wanted a divorce.

His voice was full of anger and blame. He said he could never forgive things I had said during counseling. I thought we had moved past his indiscretions. I believed we would grow old together and enjoy this new season of life.

At the time, I was visiting my mother, having just completed training in a nearby state for a health and wellness modality. My heart was pounding. My head ached. I was so grateful to have a friend I could call—someone who gently guided me through a panic attack.

Then came the emails. Ultimatums. If I didn't accept his settlement offer within 24 hours, I would get nothing.

Life didn't feel fair.

My whole identity had been rooted in my devotion to God, in service to my church, and in caring for my family. Where was God now? Why was this happening?

Within weeks, I had moved out, packed my belongings into storage, and gone to stay with family. I was still in shock. And yet... a deep peace quietly accompanied each painful step.

I remembered: in past trials—raising children, car accidents, financial loss—I had never been alone. And I wasn't alone now.

It's been a few years. My life looks very different from what I imagined. But here I am.

My life coach asked, "What are your goals—career, create income?" I said, "I don't have any right now." She replied, "Are you okay with that?" And I answered, "Today, I am."

That's when it struck me: I really *am* okay. Through God's love, I am stronger, more whole, and more aligned with my purpose.

Every decision I've made has been guided. Not right or wrong—they just were.

I'm still here.

I'm still standing.

I'm not alone.

And I'll continue forward with the same clarity, peace, and love.

"God is within her, she will not fall; God will help her at break of day."

— Psalm 46:5

74

Where the Light Leads

I've always had a connection to nature. As a kid, I'd retreat to a patch of peony bushes and just sit there. I didn't know the word meditate then—but that's what I was doing. I would watch ants crawl on the peony buds in spring, or notice how pinecones opened and closed with the weather. Everything seemed alive and somehow sacred.

One day, when I was about eight, I saw a ball of light in the woods. I approached it, and in the center of that light was a figure that looked like the pictures of Mother Mary from Sunday School. She didn't speak, but I felt complete love and acceptance. I didn't tell anyone. It felt too special—too real to explain.

A few days later, walking home from school, I found a set of beads on the ground. At the end was a medal with an image I recognized—it was Mary. I didn't know what the beads were called, or that there were prayers to say, but I instinctively held them. And holding them felt holy.

My parents are Christian—my dad, very strictly so—but I never connected with the idea of a God who micromanages or would send His son to die for me. Even with all their rules, I never doubted my parents' love. That's how I imagined God should feel, too.

In high school, I started searching for a spiritual path that reflected what I believed. I related more and more to Mother Mary, even though my parents were uncomfortable with that. I had a little statue of her in my room, and they practically thought it was the devil.

A friend introduced me to Wicca, and I attended some coven meetings. There were rituals I appreciated, but I realized I didn't want to trade one set of rules for another. Eventually, I began to shape my own spiritual path—a personal, quiet devotion to the Mother, outside of organized religion.

I don't see the vision anymore. But I still feel her. She leads me—not with commands, but with presence. Always gentle. Always guiding.

"Mary is more Mother than Queen."

— St. Thérèse of Lisieux

75

Blessed With a Life of Love

I met my husband, Bob, because I was living with his mother when he returned from four years of Army service. I had grown up on a ranch about eighteen miles outside of town. Before my junior year, I decided to work at the hospital because I had made up my mind to become a registered nurse. My family had no extra car and no money to buy one, so I planned to rent a room in town.

When my original rental fell through, Bob's mother—an RN at the hospital—invited me to stay with her. She spoke often of her son, saying he'd be coming home in August. She also wrote to him about me. When he asked, "What does she look like?" she replied, "She's blonde, short, and cute." His response? "So is a Cocker Spaniel."

Bob had once said he never intended to marry. But we celebrated his 22nd birthday together the day after he arrived. The next day, I suggested a trip to Enchanted Rock. I hadn't planned on climbing, especially in sandals, but Bob was eager. After a while, I took off my sandals and walked barefoot on the hot granite. I ended up with blisters and soaked my feet in the creek.

On the third day, he asked me to marry him. I said no—I was headed to Vanderbilt University on a nursing scholarship. Bob left to visit his dad in Del Rio, but came back the very next day. We visited every day until I left for school. Once I was gone, he wrote or sent a card *every single day*.

Six weeks later, he visited me in Nashville on his way to Fort Meade, Maryland, where he had accepted a job with the NSA as a Vietnamese linguist. He asked me again to marry him. I still wasn't ready. My plans were clear—four years of nursing school and then a career. But Bob kept calling, nearly every day.

At Thanksgiving, I couldn't afford to fly home, so Bob sent me a ticket to visit him in Baltimore. We talked a lot—about life, about love, about our dreams. In January, he sent another ticket. That time, he gave me a ring and asked again. I said yes. But then came his next question: would I give up my scholarship so we could marry in June?

I didn't say yes immediately. I prayed, wrestled, and finally—with a gentle God-nudge—I agreed. It was not an easy decision. I had worked for that scholarship since my freshman year in high school.

In March, we made our wedding plans. On a trip back to Texas, Bob's car was badly damaged in an accident. However, the repair shop understood his urgency and completed the job on time. We were married on June 6, 1970—with two ministers, just to be sure it was doubly blessed.

We moved to Baltimore. Bob continued his work at NSA, and I completed my nursing education at Johns Hopkins in 1973.

We had no formal dating period—just letters and deep conversations. Every day of our married life began the same way: Bob would say, "Good morning, beautiful. I love you."

We were blessed with two sons and a lifetime of love. For two people who hadn't planned to marry, our union could only have been arranged by God.

God transitioned Bob in November of 2014. But our souls remain forever connected—in spirit, always.

"And now these three remain: faith, hope, and love. But the greatest of these is love."

— 1 Corinthians 13:13

76

Wisdom Beyond Her Years

After a few years of marriage, we decided to expand our family. My husband and I had trouble conceiving. I prayed that if God would bless me with a child, I promised I would teach them about God. Two years later, we welcomed Sophie into our life. She would become our greatest blessing and teacher, but also our greatest challenge.

When Sophie, our daughter, was about 5 years old, our cat went missing. Sometimes, our cat, Zoe, would slip out, but she would always return by evening. One time, the cat did not return. When we prayed that night, Sophie asked God to bring Zoe back. In the morning, Zoe had not returned, and at breakfast, when we said grace, Sophie asked God again to please bring Zoe back. This went on for several days. My husband and I searched for the cat. We put up signs and went to the shelter. There was no sign of Zoe. My husband gently tried to explain to Sophie that Zoe may not come home. Sophie was not deterred, and every time a prayer was said at meals or bedtime, Sophie asked God for Zoe. After church on Sunday, Sophie asked the pastor to also ask God to help bring Zoe back home. Our pastor knelt down to Sophie's level and said a prayer. He also assured Sophie that God indeed heard her prayer. When we arrived home from church, Zoe was waiting for us on the back porch. We discovered that our neighbor was out of town for a few days, and when she came home, Zoe ran out of her garage.

Fast forward to the 4th grade. Sophie had challenges in school. She was smart, strong-willed, and opinionated. She would come home complaining that school was a waste of time. Her teachers were equally frustrated. Sophie caught on quickly. She did well on tests, but we could not get her to do her homework. She said she already knew how to do it and did not see the benefit of repeating it over and over. My husband and I had a talk with her. We both were exasperated. Finally, my husband said in his most stern voice, "School is your job! There is nothing more important to you than school!!" Sophie's eyes widened in disbelief. "You're wrong!! Daddy, how can you say that?!? There is nothing more important than God!!" and she ran off to her room. How do you reply to that when you know she has spoken the truth?

Sophie, now 14 years old, continues to be devoted to God, and her faith shines through in all that she does. She often volunteers at local homeless shelters, eager to lend a helping hand and show compassion to those in need. Her kindness doesn't stop there; she is also a fierce advocate for her peers, always standing up for those who are bullied at school, embodying the values she has learned about love and acceptance.

It amazes me how much of sacred scripture she can quote and how deeply she integrates those lessons into her life. Sophie remains our greatest blessing, a teacher of empathy and strength, and indeed, our greatest challenge. Her strong-willed nature constantly prompts us to reflect on our values and beliefs, reminding us that the journey of parenting is as much about learning from her as it is about guiding her. In every prayer and every act of kindness, we see the profound impact of her faith, and we are incredibly grateful for the powerful presence she is in our lives.

"...and a little child shall lead them."

— Isaiah 11:6

77

Listening For God

I have spent my entire life talking to and praying to God. At sixty-four years of age that is a lot of talking and a lot of praying – all that went unanswered.

It is because of God's silence that I began to question his very existence. "How can there truly be a higher power at work that can't even take the time to talk with me? To answer a prayer?" The answer had to be simple. There is no God.

It was at this time that my moment of clarity hit me. While it is true that God never parted the clouds and yelled down to me, "I am here! I am listening!" God was still with me.

I was too consumed with waiting for the booming voice from the heavens that I realized that I had missed a lifetime of God's whispers to me.

God was with me in my first car, helping me become a better driver – he needed to be there, too.

He was there at my wedding, the birth of my children, the baptisms, the birthday parties. He was there for it all.

He was the gentle breeze and the warm sun on my face on a beautiful spring day. He was the magical feelings and joy in every Christmas light.

God was with my family and I when my mother died. It was God that held her hand while I held the other.

I see God in the eyes of my children, and I see him in the lives of my growing grandchildren. He has given me the gift to see the lives of my family that will go on when I am gone.

While it is true that God has never talked with me the way people do, he has been busy moving through my life the entire time. I just didn't realize it.

I realize it now. I now devote the quiet moments in my life to the one thing I can now understand. I am no longer listening for God.

I am listening TO God.

"And after the fire came a gentle whisper."

— 1 Kings 19:12

78

The Presence of the Mother

The first time I saw the young mother, she was pushing her baby in a stroller up the street. Phone in hand, earbuds secure, she navigated the stroller with a few fingers. I saw her again the next day and the next. Always, phone in hand. Earbuds in place. Navigating the stroller with a few fingers. She seemed to me a little . . . detached.

One day, my daughter and I drove up the street on our way to the store. We spotted the young mother. She was strolling her baby down the center of the road, phone in hand. Earbuds in place.

"Honk," my cranky daughter said. "Oh my God, how irresponsible! What kind of mother is she?"

To counter my daughter's anger, I said, "It's okay. She will move."

And the young mother did move. As our car drew closer, she heard us through the earbuds and moved out of the road. Still, my thought bubble would have conveyed: "You really need to get off your phone and pay attention."

As my daughter had said, "What kind of mother is she?"

Yesterday I was walking the dog. Halfway through the walk, I heard a gentle voice from behind. The voice was so incredibly kind, soft, and nurturing.

"Yes," she was cooing, "you see the puppy?" I heard the perky babbling of a toddler. With her sweet words, the woman responded to whatever the toddler had said, and I thought, "Wow, this woman has the most wonderful motherly presence I've ever felt."

I turned around, and there she was. Pushing the stroller with two fingers. Phone in hand. Earbuds secure.

Without my eyes deceiving me, all I could hear were her words; all I could feel was her presence. It was pure love. Being in front of her like that, not being able to see her, had replicated the baby's experience for me.

He couldn't SEE his mother or the other things that captured her attention.

But he could HEAR his mother. He could FEEL his mother.

In this same way, we sometimes question whether the Holy Spirit is with us. What kind of Mother is she? Through silent meditation, we can hear the Mother's voice and feel her presence. But in the hullabaloo of the bustling world, sometimes we forget. Although we cannot see her with our eyes, she is there effortlessly, moving us along, assuring us when we are troubled, and keeping us safe.

But the Comforter, which is the Holy Ghost, whom the Father will send in my name, shall teach you all things, and bring all things to your remembrance, whatsoever I have said unto you. Peace I leave with you, my peace I give unto you: not as the world giveth, give I unto you. Let not your heart be troubled, neither let it be afraid.

--1 John 14: 26-27

79

Lefty's Lesson: Finding Freedom in Surrender

I had a cat named Lefty. One day, I was unloading bags from a trip to the store, and Lefty became curious and started nosing around in the empty plastic bags that I'd tossed aside. She was having a great time until she turned around inside one of the bags. One of her hind legs was stuck inside the handle hole. She tried to walk away, immediately noticing the weird *tch-tch-tch* sound following her. With every step, she dragged the bag behind her. The loud, crinkly noise scared her so much that, yes, she tried to run away from it.

But she couldn't run away from it. Her leg was hooked in there, and the noise followed her as she darted around the apartment, the panic and chaos increasing the faster she ran.

(Through stifled laughter), I kept reaching out and saying, "Lefty, stop, let me help you."

The problem was that I couldn't help her, not as long as she was in a panic and darting back and forth. I couldn't help her until she got tired and stopped.

I found her in the closet, out of breath, and hunkered in the corner in fear. I gently unhooked the bag from her leg.

Without the scary thing following her around, Lefty went back to normal. She just needed to stop, surrender, and trust. And she was saved through no effort of her own. We do this, too. Both things, known and unknown, frighten us, and we panic. We may run from our problems and, in our fear of losing the battle, become trapped in our own chaos. Eventually, we grow weary of all the ruckus, and we stop and surrender to the help of a Higher Power. Through this vulnerability, we are free.

And call on me in the day of trouble; I will deliver you, and you will honor me.

— Psalm 50:15

80

No Man's Land: A Magical Escape

One night at the Kibbutz, shortly after the Six-Day War between Israel and the Arab states, I decided to take a walk by the river as darkness fell. While humming the song "The River Jordan," I suddenly felt a tap on my shoulder. Turning around, I was confronted by a dark-skinned man with a gun aimed at me. He spoke limited English and asked what I was doing. I had unknowingly wandered into a military no man's land between Jordan and Israel.

The man forced me to walk towards a military watchtower in the distance, rifle still trained on me. When we arrived, I saw another soldier inside, who looked even more intimidating as he loaded his rifle. Fear gripped me, and I braced myself for the worst. In that moment, I remembered I had a magic trick in my pocket—a black wooden paddle. Taking a gamble, I decided to perform the trick.

To my relief, a smile broke across their faces, which soon turned into laughter and amazement as they examined the result of my performance. What began as a terrifying encounter transformed into a fragile friendship. They explained that the area was a minefield, and I was lucky to have escaped unharmed. They guided me through the minefield and showed me a barbed wire fence I needed to crawl under. I followed their instructions and made my way back to the Kibbutz through the darkness. It seemed that magic truly had saved my life that night.

"The Lord will keep you from all harm—He will watch over your life."

— Psalm 121:7

81

A Father's Love: Daniel's Short Life

Our first son, Daniel Adam, was born on December 17th, 1979. It was not an easy birth; he was delivered via forceps, but I was present for the whole miraculous event. After about three weeks, Carol struggled a bit with breastfeeding, and I noticed that Daniel's face appeared slightly blue and swollen. We drove him to our local clinic for a check-up, where we were informed that he had a potential heart issue and needed to go to the hospital. That night turned into a nightmare. A very nice doctor in a suit soon arrived, and within minutes, our little boy was covered in various tubes connected to machines. It was a heartbreaking sight, and we had no idea what was wrong. He was diagnosed with a very rare heart condition and underwent an operation. We were told it should work for a year or so, but he would need another surgery afterward. That year was tough, filled with many visits to doctors and hospitals. He was on several medications that we administered through a syringe.

During this time, I found a job at an unusual venue called "Shakespeare's Tavern and Playhouse" in the city of London, near St. Paul's Cathedral. After a few months, the management asked me to create a large-scale medieval magic and illusion show, building a stage specifically to my specifications. It was a fantastic opportunity, even though I had to file a case to recover my full paycheck. This experience led to another contract at a different venue, resulting in a relatively high salary.

As my time at "Shakespeare's Tavern and Playhouse" came to an end, Daniel was due for his major operation. His doctor performed a "Switch" operation, making him a pioneer in this field, as such procedures would become more commonplace in the future. After several hours of anxious waiting in the waiting room, my sister Hilary arrived just before the doctor entered to inform us that Daniel had survived the surgery but was on life support. We watched the monitor as his heartbeat eventually flatlined, and our little boy passed into the next world.

About ten minutes later, after they had removed all his tubes, we were allowed to see him. He lay on his back, holding a white rose, looking like an angel. With my arm around Carol, amidst our tears, I looked up to the ceiling and felt his presence looking down on us. I knew he was at peace. He died on March 10th, 1981.

"He will wipe every tear from their eyes. There will be no more death or mourning or crying or pain, for the old order of things has passed away."

— *Revelation 21:4*

82

Holding On: In the Company of Shadows

Sometimes, I wonder if my memory is a gift or a trickster—always showing me snapshots like old Polaroids in a shoebox, soft at the edges, smudged but glowing. Some memories hum like lullabies. Others scream like sirens in the middle of the night. But I keep holding them. All of them. Because they are mine.

I remember the way the screen door slammed when someone came in too fast. The smell of damp laundry when it rained for too many days in a row. I remember the taste of metal that came from the green hose that lay near my swings. I remember when it was hot and the way the sky turned yellow before a storm. It was like the world was holding its breath.

And the silence after Jimmy, my brother, died— how even the house stopped making its usual sounds. I remember trying to listen for him in the spaces between the ticking of the clock and the buzzing of the porch light. I thought maybe if I was really still, I could hear his voice in the wind, or maybe he'd whisper something in a dream. Sarah, too—Jimmy's girlfriend...her laugh used to bounce off the walls. Then nothing. Just stillness. A haunting kind of still. After that, time lost its color for a while. I moved in a fog. I sat in classrooms and stared through the teachers. I smiled when I was supposed to. I said fine when asked. I walked home the long way so I didn't have to pretend. I started to disappear from the inside out. Sometimes, I think I evaporated a little. But I never fully vanished. Not completely. There were people who tried to erase me. With words. With hands. With silence. There were days when I wanted to forget how to speak, how to feel, how to be. But even in those moments, something inside me whispered, "Hold on." It wasn't loud, but it was there. It was God. Or the Brook Troll. Or Jimmy. Or all three. I don't need to know. I just know it kept me alive. My body became a battleground, though... Food. Pills. Secrets. Shame. I tried to control the outside so I didn't have to feel the storm inside. I starved, and I binged. I hid, and I hustled. I said yes when I wanted to scream no. I disappeared in plain sight. And still, I held on. The moon always knew. So did the wind. They never judged me. They just were. Quiet. Watching. Accepting. The Son ... Jesus would touch my skin and remind me I was still here, still breathing, still capable of feeling warmth. Even when it hurt.

And then, I started to remember myself. Not all at once. Not in some cinematic breakthrough. Just piece by piece. A poem here. A walk alone there. A breath. A moment of real laughter. In time, I said no and meant it. I started to let love in. Little bits at first, then more. And then I started giving it back. Carefully. Then Fiercely. I started mothering my younger self. Sitting with her. Holding her hand. Letting her cry. Letting her rage. I let her tell the truth—our truth. And I didn't turn away.

Now, I don't need to be perfect. I don't even want to be. I want to be real. I want to live with my whole heart cracked wide open and still beating. I want to sit beside the brook and talk to the wind and sing to the trees and tell the stars that I made it. I made it! And I am still making it. Every freaking day. I am living proof that the light of the Son never leaves, even when we forget how to see.

"The light shines in the darkness, and the darkness has not overcome it."

— John 1:5

83

A Cat's Tale: An Angel Sent from Heaven

It has been a year since my Russian Blue cat, Boris, passed away. This past spring, my great-aunt passed on. It was a hot summer day in June. I had left work and was on my way to my Great-Aunt's house to feed the neighborhood cats. There are fourteen cats. I put out the food and got in my car.

I have the radio on and am driving to my home. While in my car, I hear a meow sound. I stopped at the CVS drive-thru to get my prescription. All of a sudden, I hear a " meow" sound again. I am surprised to hear that. I drive around the corner in my townhouse. I got out of the car and saw a little kitten in the wheel well.

I called my mom on the phone and told her there was a kitten on the wheel of my car. To the rescue, she and my stepdad Dave came over to pull out the kitten. It is a Russian blue cat, just like my cat Boris. The kitten has the same markings as my cat Boris. The kitten has survived a fifteen-mile drive from Kansas City to a suburb in the wheel of my car. She was taken to a vet and was fine. She just had a little hernia. We named her Milagro, which means "miracle" in Spanish, and we call her Milly for short.

Milly was taken to my mom's house, since I could not have pets at my house. I think my cat Boris from above sent Milly to bring joy into a stressful time. An angel sent from heaven. The cat I loved today was sent by the cat I loved yesterday. Milly will always hold a special place in my heart.

May the God of hope fill you with all joy and peace in believing, so that by the power of the holy spirit you may abound in hope.
— *Romans 15:13*

84

A Feline Connection Bridging Two Worlds

When I worked as a home health nurse, I would visit patients and check in on them. Depending on the person's needs, I would dress wounds, give insulin injections, and teach them about their medications and disease processes, and when to seek help. I would travel all over the county to many different socio-economic areas, but my favorite was the projects. This is where I felt I made the greatest impact.

One time, as I was walking up to see a patient, I saw three teenage boys tossing a small cat onto the roof and knocking it off with a broom. I walked over to them, and as one of the boys caught it coming off the roof, I asked him if I could hold it. When I held it, it immediately calmed down, and I quit crying. "Who does this kitty belong to?" I asked.

They started answering: "Aww, no one, we can't have pets here." "It is just a pest," "All it does is cry," "It just wants to eat." "It's not good for anything."

As the boys were telling me these things about the cat, in my heart, I heard people saying the same things about them. I asked them if I could have this kitten. They responded, "Sure," "Good Riddance!"

This kitty became the cat of my life. Then, each time I saw these boys, they would call out, "Hey, Yo! Still got that cat?" It was more like a greeting of "Hi, How are you?" Over the next months, I would show them pictures of the cat sleeping or doing crazy kitty things. I would bring them apples or candy bars. They would sit on my car, protecting it, while I saw my patient.

One afternoon, when I got home from work, this cat ran outside in front of me and was hit and killed by a car. I was heartbroken. I could hardly stop crying.

The next day, the boys were in their gathering place. When one calls out, "Hey! Yo! Got that cat?" I couldn't hold back the tears. These boys gathered around me, asking what was wrong. I told them that the cat was hit by a car and died. They each gave me big hugs, and one of the boys promised that if they ever found another cat, they would save it for me.

"The Lord is good to all; he has compassion on all he has made."

— Psalm 145:9

85

In The Arms of Jesus

The day was September 11, 2001. The day started with an absolutely beautiful, clear blue sky. Who knew that the day would soon begin with one of the most horrendous terrorist attacks witnessed by mankind. I had accompanied a friend who was wheelchair-bound to an awards breakfast, where she was honored for being the chosen artist for the front cover of the booklet and posters for the annual charity campaign that federal employees can contribute to. We never witnessed the award ceremony, as everything stopped after whispers in the ears of those running the ceremony.

We were then told there was a possible attack on the U.S. and that we should leave. We encountered intense traffic trying to get me back to where my car was parked by our work building, which is usually a 5-minute drive, but it took us over 2 hours. By then, I needed to go into the building briefly, but I ended up staying longer in my office because there were so many cars trying to evacuate the area. As a few other co-workers and I watched the replay of the attacks on the Twin Towers in NY on TV, we only left when our deputy director came into our room and told us to leave. My normal 15 to 20-minute drive home lasted over 3 hours.

While on the long, traffic-filled, slow ride home, I found myself feeling immense sorrow and compassion for all those who had died, especially those who jumped from the buildings. I began to pray for all who died so suddenly, and I cried out to Jesus, "What if they were not ready to go to Heaven?" Jesus immediately showed Himself standing in front of the tower buildings with His arms outstretched, catching all of those who were falling. Then I heard Him say: "Murder is the worst thing that could happen to a soul, and therefore, I took them all up into My arms." He then asked me not to pray for all those who died as He was taking care of them, but instead to pray for the comfort, love, and strength that would be needed by all of their loved ones left behind. Jesus's words gave me immediate comfort.

A few weeks later, I was walking in the hallways of the school at church and noticed the youth ministry board had a picture posted that illustrated exactly what Jesus had described to me! I felt that spiritual tingling all down my spine that happens when something is so true. I asked to make a copy of the picture, and I have had it at my desk at work ever since, as well as on our refrigerator at home, so I can continually be reminded of the great hope that Jesus's love gives us. I eventually found out that the picture was drawn by an 8– or 9–year-old the day after the tragic events after their teacher encouraged her students to draw what they felt about what had happened the day before. When you think about it, it was an additional miracle, given that we were in the relatively early years of the Internet, to be connected in just a few weeks after the tragic events to a child I had never met who apparently saw the same vision of Jesus as I had seen.

"Even in the darkest moments, love gives hope."

— St. John Paul II (2001 address after 9/11)

86

Jesus Meets Us Where We Are

One day, I was drawn to visit a Catholic church that appeared to minister to a predominantly Korean community on my way home from a doctor's appointment I had not visited before. Upon entering the church sanctuary, I saw a crucifix at the center of the altar that showed Jesus very graphically with the signs of his immense suffering from the crucifixion. Immediately, I felt intense sadness and began to cry, thinking of how much Jesus had suffered despite the many years I had spent before that day contemplating all that He went through. I began to think of other churches I had been in where the crucifix was not as graphic, or instead showed Jesus in the resurrected form in front of the cross. Then I thought of the Korean people, their culture, and how amazing it was that some of them had accepted Christianity as their faith and worship. While I had heard of stories coming out of North Korea of Christians being staked alive in front of their fellow villagers, that helped me understand the focus on Jesus's suffering, but I was not sure that Koreans from South Korea would necessarily focus so intently on His suffering upon the cross. I asked Jesus if He had meant for us to focus on His suffering for over 2000 years and not as much on His Resurrection. I felt Jesus say: No, he had not meant for that, and that he had meant for everyone to be free to experience the Ascension as He had. He then explained that, despite this, He meets all of them where they are in their faith journey and gently brings them a step forward in understanding His true mission of coming to Earth. I walked out of that church that day, marveling at

Jesus' great love and acceptance for each person by meeting them where they are in their spiritual growth journey.

"Where there is injury, let me sow pardon; where there is doubt, faith; where there is despair, hope; where there is darkness, light."

— St Francis of Assisi

87

Jesus's Ever-Present Love

On Christmas Eve 2015, before falling asleep, I thought of Jesus as the newborn infant in the manger and asked Him, "What gift can I give You, my Sweet Jesus?" He responded, "Carry Me in your heart! Carry Me in your heart, and I will always be with you! I will always shine in your heart! Our hearts shine together!"

At that moment, I envisioned myself embracing Him as an infant, feeling His great light shining deep into my heart and entire being. Tears flowed down my cheeks as I heard and felt His response. I realized that carrying Him in my heart would allow me to always experience Divine Love, Light, Peace, Joy, and Hope, not only within myself but also in how I see the world. Anyone who has held a child close to their heart and chest knows this feeling, even if they do not have the words to express it.

"Abide in me, and I in you."

— John 15:4

88

Angels Surrounding Us

I was about a third of the way through my pregnancy with my son when, one day, after a music liturgy meeting at church, I left to drive home. I came upon an intersection with a traffic light. However, after noticing the light was green, and other cars in front of me were still going forward, I proceeded to continue going straight. Still, right in the middle of the intersection, the light suddenly turned red, and I swerved to the right to avoid being hit or hitting other cars. I saw car after car coming directly at me. I couldn't understand why I wasn't experiencing head-on crashes. I eventually ended up on the right side of the road with my car on the side in the wrong driving direction. I usually hyperventilate when getting very scared, but I was calm and not even shaking. I called my husband to explain what had just happened, but I was on my way home, and it would take me a little longer, as I was going to take the back road instead of the faster route I normally take.

Fast forward 9 years later, as I was reading another spiritual metaphysical book after the event at church where my son had seen the color changes on the priest before he passed out, I heard my son call out from his bedroom. He was seeing an angel. My mother's instinct kicked in, and I heard the angel tell me his name. I had just read about him! I then asked my son how the angel looked. He began to describe how tall he was and that he was smiling at him from a side profile. That confirmed for me that it was Archangel Sandalphon, who is described by Hebrew tradition to be as tall as from Heaven to Earth. I asked my son to ask the angel for his name. My son responded, "You know who it is, Mommy!" I pondered how my son knew I knew who the angel was and that I could hear him speak. My son saw Sandalphon over the course of a few days. Over those three days, I helped my son open his spiritual hearing so he could hear the angel speak as well. The first night, I asked my son to ask the angel for the first few sounds of his name. Then, on the second night, I asked him to ask for the last few sounds of the angel's name. By the third night, when I asked him to get the middle of the angel's name, my son could not only hear it but could hear the angel's full name and then a full conversation as well. Then he told me he saw St. Michael. I marveled at the miraculous experience and was grateful for my maternal instinct and trust in what was happening without placing judgment upon it all, given my strong Catholic upbringing. I went back to my bedroom, pleading with St. Michael, to let me see him too. All I saw were beautiful swirling colors of purple, gold, blue, and some green. I then felt drawn to ask him about the near-miss car accident event when I was pregnant with my son 9 years prior. St. Michael confirmed for me that I did see the other cars coming at me but that he and other angels had lifted up my car into a different dimension where the other cars could not see me and could not actually hit me. St. Michael then said my son and I were not meant to die that day, as he was meant to be born and was a very special gift to the world.

"The angel of the Lord encamps around those who fear him, and he delivers them."

— Psalm 34:7

89

Divinely Guided

One Sunday, my family and I decided to attend services at a Catholic Church known for its beautiful angels flanking the altar. As was our custom, we chose to sit in the front pew. My son, who was eight years old at the time, kept urging me to help. Confused, I explained that since this wasn't our regular church, I thought others had things under control. After a few more minutes, he insisted again, this time with greater urgency. I told him to be quiet since we were in the front pew.

About five minutes later, the priest came to the front of the altar to prepare for Holy Communion, and then he collapsed. At that moment, all thoughts of my son's insistence vanished as I rushed to the altar, ready to perform CPR and wondering who would call 911, given that cell phones were still new. It felt surreal; I was moving quickly while everything else seemed to slow down. I noticed someone holding a cell phone and considered how close the firehouse was to the church—less than a quarter of a mile away. Just then, I saw the priest open his eyes and understood that CPR was unnecessary.

I picked up the ciboria with the Holy Communion hosts and announced to those waiting in line that I was a Eucharistic Minister. Although I was only authorized to serve in our regular church, I told them to go ahead and receive Communion and then leave, as the priest couldn't continue Mass, and we needed to clear space for the paramedics, who I expected to arrive soon. Everyone looked at me in shock, frozen in place, including the lay Eucharistic Ministers who were supposed to assist. I repeated my message two more times, and finally, one of the ministers moved to join me. At that moment, more people seemed ready to receive Communion, but they remained quiet and stayed in their pews, waiting for the paramedics to arrive. They only left when the paramedics wheeled the priest out. Despite the carpeted floor, it was so quiet that you could have heard a pin drop—something I've never experienced before or since.

Since my family was in the front pew, we exited the church last. As we walked down the aisle, I asked my son how he knew something was going to happen. He replied, with a knowing air, that he had seen the priest's color change. I was puzzled and didn't understand what he meant at that moment. Later that day, I called my sister, who laughed and called me a "Catholic ostrich" for being so unaware. I protested, saying, "I don't care what any priest thinks about what happened. I know, with all my heart, my son did nothing wrong!" She recommended several books, mostly based on Edgar Cayce's readings. I read all of them and found others over the next eight months.

I began to realize that my son might have the gift of seeing auras. Eight months later, I sat down with him to ask some questions to confirm my thoughts. He recalled the day vividly and described how he had seen one color around the priest that then darkened or became muddied, prompting a premonition that I should go help. He felt this 20 to 25 minutes before the priest collapsed. This experience led me to understand that he could see color changes in others and had intuitive feelings about what those changes meant. We made an agreement for him to protect his gift from anyone who might tease him for it.

This beautiful gift has helped him avoid suffering during traumatic events, offered insight into when others may not be truthful, and promoted compassion for those around him. I felt grateful because, as a young mother, I was centered and confident in my son's God-given abilities, refusing to let others judge him negatively for them.

"We have different gifts, according to the grace given to each of us. If your gift is prophesying, then prophesy in accordance with your faith."

— Romans 12:6

90

A Night in the Woods

Everything seemed perfect in my life until the day it all fell apart. I had a dream job with a nice salary, a beautiful wife, three smart and talented children, an elegant home in a prestigious neighborhood, and a vacation house by the lake that we rarely visited. On top of all that, I had a young mistress on the side.

When my oldest daughter wanted to have a sleepover party with a few friends, I felt a wave of dread. I loved my children, but the last thing I wanted was to endure a chaotic night filled with shrieking teens, loud music, and endless messes. So, I told my wife that I had to be in New York for the party dates. I can still picture her sweet smile as she assured me that she could manage everything. To make things easier for her, I even offered to leave my car at the airport, giving me several days alone with my girlfriend.

On the day of the party, as my daughter's friends arrived, I kissed my wife and girls goodbye and told them I was sorry to miss it but to have a great party; I would see them on Sunday. Little did I know my wife planned to take the girls to the lake house. I picked up my girlfriend and drove off to the lake house.

We were enjoying ourselves when we heard the happy laughter of kids coming into the house. The look of pain and shock on everyone's face was one I will never forget. My life changed completely, and it was my own doing. I lost my wife, and my relationship with my children was severely damaged. My girlfriend lost interest as soon as she realized I was trying to explain her to my wife.

While my wife initially agreed to counseling, the shattered trust was too difficult to repair. My career was on shaky ground, and I was urged to take a few weeks off to get myself together. During that time, I made the lake house my home. It was set in a secluded area next to a vast wooded preserve. One evening, just before dusk, I decided to take a walk in the woods, coming to terms with the man I had become.

I don't know how long I had walked when I realized it was dark. I turned to go home, and on the way back, I tripped and twisted my ankle. The pain shot through my leg, making it impossible to hobble more than a few feet at a time. I remembered I had left my phone at home on the charger. I was alone, cold, scared, and surrounded by the darkness.

Overwhelmed and exhausted, I collapsed to the ground and started praying, whispering, "I'm Sorry, I'm Sorry, I'm Sorry." It was like surrendering, and love and peace came over me.

I fell asleep, and when I woke up, the sun was coming through the leaves, and I felt the peace continue to be with me. My ankle was swollen, but I was able to find my way limping back to the house. From that moment, things have slowly improved little by little. But that feeling of peace and love that surrounded me that night in the woods has never completely left. I know that whatever I have to face, the presence of love will always be with me.

"Rock bottom became the solid foundation on which I rebuilt my life."

— J.K. Rowling

91

2B or Not 2B: A Journey of Healing

I was guided to go to Sedona during COVID in June of 2020 to assist and be a part of a spiritual community. Things had fallen apart in my primary relationships, and I yearned to be with people who understood me. Instead, I discovered the 12 steps of Co-Dependency and finished all of them in just six months. I decided to fully embrace step 12 and go back and repair the relationships I had left behind.

Before I left, a friend of mine suggested writing my angels, asking for guidance on the signs I should look for as I embarked on this journey. I decided to request a series of repeating numbers: 222, 333, 444, and 555. The months spent back home were incredibly challenging as I was going through a divorce while facing my family's discontent. Yet, amidst it all, I began to see the number 222 everywhere. It brought me a sense of comfort and reassurance.

Once my divorce was final, I decided to return to Sedona, believing I still had significant work to do there. I found a residence in Cottonwood, where I lived for six months in apartment #2. At the time, I didn't think much of this number, but as we know, God's timing is not our own. I found employment transporting the elderly to their appointments and working in a call center. One day, I noticed that the building number at my workplace was 2. Once again, it didn't click, and I continued with my routine.

Eventually, I relocated to Sedona after a miracle of sorts. I was the only one to show up for a rental, and the landlord decided to take a chance on me without considering any other applicants. I moved into a house that was divided into three units, and of course, I was in the second unit. One day, it suddenly dawned on me that all these occurrences of the number 2 added up to 222. This realization was a profound affirmation that I was on the right path, and it was during the year 2022 that this insight was fully revealed to me.

Fast forward three years, and I am still amazed at the growth I've experienced while living in Arizona. My relationships have flourished in ways I can only describe as miraculous. I feel truly blessed, and this journey has reminded me that we are never alone if we choose to open our hearts to the love that surrounds us.

The number 222 symbolizes the need for balance in various aspects of life, including relationships, work, and personal well-being. It serves as a reminder that peace is achieved when we cultivate balance in our daily routines. Additionally, angel number 222 often appears when it's time to focus on partnerships, whether romantic, familial, or professional. It's a gentle nudge to nurture our connections and create meaningful bonds.

In moments when life feels overwhelming or uncertain, the appearance of 222 reassures us to trust the process. It's a message from our angels, urging us to remain patient and have faith that everything is unfolding as it should. Lastly, the number 222 embodies the energy of manifestation. If you find yourself seeing this number frequently, it's a strong signal to maintain positive thoughts and align with your goals, as they are beginning to take form.

"When the soul is ready, the path appears."

— Author

92

Misfit's Journey to Belonging

Over the past few years, I became "different." I no longer felt comfortable with my friends. I didn't believe what they believed. I had never enjoyed playing or watching team sports, but now they seemed downright dull. When I was invited to Super Bowl parties, I would politely decline and could usually be found reading a book or out on a walk. At New Year's Eve parties, I found myself bored, watching others become intoxicated.

I worked in data entry, transitioned to IT support, and eventually became an administrative assistant, but each of these jobs soon became repetitive and unfulfilling.

Though I believed in God and had accepted Jesus as my Savior in my youth, I sensed there was more to being a Christian than going to church or saying grace before meals. I just didn't know how to reach that *more*.

What I did know was that it wasn't found in Sunday church services.

At just 32, I wasn't depressed, but I felt stuck—so I decided to see a therapist. In her office, one of the decorations caught my eye. It read: "Blessed are the weird people—poets, misfits, writers, mystics, painters, troubadours—for they teach us to see the world through different eyes."

I shared how I felt out of place, how the things most people seemed to enjoy left me feeling empty.

To help me explore new paths, my therapist encouraged me to write down five things I was grateful for each day. She also arranged for me to volunteer with Meals on Wheels, delivering food to homebound seniors once a week. To my surprise, I found deep joy in those simple interactions. I felt a kind of fulfillment I hadn't experienced in years.

A few months later, a position opened in one of their offices. I applied but wasn't chosen. Though I was disappointed, they said they'd keep my resume on file. Not long after, I received a call about a case manager role involving direct client contact. I eagerly accepted—and soon realized how much I loved the work.

When I shared this with my therapist, I told her, "I think this is my calling." She gently replied, "Perhaps this is how you're fulfilling your calling right now. But remember—a job, even one that helps others, isn't necessarily the calling. Serving others is the calling."

That evening, driving home, something shifted. I no longer felt like a misfit. I realized I *do* belong—just not in the places I was looking before. I could almost hear Jesus say, 'You were never lost; you were being set apart.'

"Truly I tell you, whatever you did for one of the least of these brothers and sisters of mine, you did for me."

— Matthew 25:40

93

Courage in the Cafeteria

When I went into the cafeteria, a bunch of the popular mean girls were surrounding Lily. They were bullying her, dumping her milk on her, laughing at her. Lily had a birthmark on her face, and the mean girls made fun of her. She tried to leave, but they blocked her way. Watching this, I felt sick to my stomach.

I could hear what they were saying about how the spilled milk made her look better. It was disgusting. I had never really spoken up before, but something in me snapped. With my heart pounding, I pushed through the crowd. "What's your problem?" I blurted out, and the laughter stopped me, and everyone stared at me.

"Newsflash: being 'pretty' doesn't give you the right to put others down or make them feel bad. It just makes you pathetic!" One of the girls started to say something, but before she could, I shouted at her, "It's easy to tear someone down when you think it makes you look better. But let me tell you, the real strength lies in lifting each other up, not in pointing out flaws." I was ready to say more, but several teachers were there to break us up. We all ended up in the principal's office.

The mean girls claimed it was an accident that milk got spilled on Lily. I spoke up again. I said it wasn't an accident. They did it on purpose. I realized I might have crossed a line, but it felt right to stand up for Lily.

Sure enough, the principal called each of our parents. Even though Lily and my parents were called, neither one of us got in trouble.

Even though I felt scared, I knew it was the right thing to do. My dad said he was proud of me and that sometimes, all it takes is one voice to make a difference. I think it has given me the courage to do it again if I need to.

"He has shown you, O mortal, what is good. And what does the Lord require of you? To act justly and to love mercy and to walk humbly with your God."

— Micah 6:8

94

An Instrument of Love

I was bullied all through school. I was the last one picked, called cruel names, pushed at the bus stop, and had my hair yanked more times than I could count. Often, I had to stand on the bus because no one would let me sit. Even at the skating rink, I was knocked off my feet.

One day in middle school, the girls were at it again. I could see Patricia about to join in, swept up in the crowd. But her mother, *Mrs. B*, was nearby. She stepped in—firm, clear, and loving.

"You are not going to do that," she told her daughter. "You're going to be that girl's friend. You're going to be her best friend."

And Patricia was. She still is.

Though we live miles apart now, I know she loves me. And only a few years ago, I found out what her mother had said that day. I had no idea. I just knew that someone had stepped into the dark and shone a light. A kindness I needed then—and still carry with me now.

Parents can be instrumental in a child's life… sometimes, even a child who isn't their own.

Today, I told Patricia to hug her mom for me. To say thank you.

Her mother's kindness made her a heroine in my eyes.

So if you see something—if you see someone hurting—step in. Don't let the pain continue. Be a helper. Be a healer. Be an instrument of love in this world.

"Therefore, as God's chosen people, holy and dearly loved, clothe yourselves with compassion, kindness, humility, gentleness and patience."

— Colossians 3:12

95

The Arrow of Light

It was a fine spring morning in Dallas, Texas, when I climbed into a dusty old van parked outside a church. I didn't know it then, but this would be one of the most spiritual and terrifying experiences of my life. Jim and Bill, two guys I barely knew but felt strangely drawn to, climbed in beside me. We laughed, made jokes, and had no idea what we were stepping into. Five more people climbed into the van. Someone passed around caramel popcorn packages.

We were headed for a cave in the cliffs along the Texas stretch of the Colorado River near Lampasas, Texas. The plan was simple—explore, have fun, and get a little muddy. Nothing about it seemed dangerous at the time. When we arrived, the group leader tossed some rocks into the cave's entrance to make sure no bears had made it their home. It was a moment of caution that, in hindsight, felt almost ceremonial, like knocking on the door of another world.

We entered the cave cautiously, trying to keep our shoes dry and our spirits high. Soon, though, we surrendered to the inevitable—our feet were soaked, and mud clung to our legs. We each carried carbide gas lamps that hissed and burned with a soft, ghostly glow. I had little experience with spelunking and even less understanding of the dangers that might await underground.

As we ventured deeper, we began to notice something strange. We were panting. Our breath came quicker and shallower. The air felt thick, wrong somehow. Someone struck a match—and it fizzled out instantly. That was our warning: the air was low on oxygen, likely laced with dangerous gas. But, like fools—or perhaps like pilgrims under a spell—we pressed on.

Water rose to our knees, then higher. Still, we trudged forward. After about thirty minutes, we squeezed through two narrow rock gaps, forcing our bodies through stone-like toothpaste. Fifteen minutes later, we reached a dead end. We had no choice but to turn back.

As we retraced our steps, Jim and Bill suddenly veered off into a side passage. I called after them, warned them, and told them it was a bad idea. But something pulled me—a protective instinct, maybe something deeper—and I followed. The water was waist-high now, murky and cold. Every step felt like a question: *What lies beneath this surface? Could there be a drop-off? A shaft?* I asked if they could swim. Neither of them could.

We kept going. The passage seemed endless, a watery tunnel of stone and silence. Then it hit us—we were lost.

No one knew where we were. No one would hear us call. The lights hissed in the gas-thick air. Time stretched. I thought of how easy it would be to disappear in a place like this, how many had before. My heart pounded with both fear and something else: a kind of surrender. This might be it.

But just when our hope was wearing thin, the miracle happened.

There, in the flickering light of our lamps, was an arrow. Spray-painted on the cave wall. An arrow pointing the way out. It may have been put there by a previous group, but in that moment, it was more than paint. It was a message. It was guidance. It was divine.

That arrow became the most beautiful thing I had ever seen.

Minutes later, light from the outside world appeared like a halo in the darkness. We scrambled forward, and then, at last, we emerged. The sun hit my face like a blessing. I wanted to kiss the ground. Maybe I should have. I knew—*we all knew*—we had come close to death.

But something greater had reached into that darkness and shown us the way.

To this day, I believe that God inspired whoever painted that arrow. It wasn't just a mark on a wall. It was a message of grace. A promise that even in the deepest, most gas-filled caverns of fear and confusion—if you keep walking, if you stay open—there will be light. There will be a way out.

"At the moment when all seems lost, and your strength is gone, help will come."

— White Eagle

96

There Are Angels on Earth, After All

I am a true believer in God extending a helping hand when you need it the most, and He does so in unexpected ways, too. My heart swells with gratitude whenever I recall the mysterious ways the "divine one" has helped me.

This little snippet is my humble attempt to express my eternal gratitude to the one person who has given me the help I needed when I needed it the most. Her name is Latha, whom we always called "Lathamma" as a sign of respect, as per our local cultural norm in India.

In an era where kindness is a rarity and selfless service is forgotten, Lathamma embodies that in every form. My family and friends who have known me for decades are aware that I have had to take charge of the complete care of my beloved late father, who was a chronic kidney disease patient. Lathamma was my Dad's housekeeper for a few years before he was diagnosed. She was one among many since my Dad has been a widower since the year 1992 after my mom passed away from a sudden case of bronchitis at the very young age of 45.

Since her passing, my Dad had many housekeepers running the home when he worked, but Lathamma, for some strange reason, came a few years before his diagnosis and stayed through the good and the next few bad years of his life as a CKD patient before his passing in 2020.

Lathamma had a family of 5 at home, but she still came to help with my Dad's care after my Dad's kidney failure diagnosis in the year

2016. To give you her background, Lathamma, unlike many in the lower strata of low-income families in India, was actually educated till Grade 10. She met the love of her life and married him when she turned 18 and dedicated her life to taking care of her kids. She is a woman of strength when I say she endured her fair share of tribulations during the same time as my father's illness. What makes me eternally grateful to her is that in 2017, she lost her 2nd son to a terrible road accident, and in 2019, her eldest son had a rare form of meningitis. She grieved for her loss like any mother does, but her unwavering service to my Dad continued even during these times of sadness. She always treated my father like her very own Dad, whom she lost when she was in her early teens. My Dad considered her his daughter as well and showered her with praise when needed, compassion in a thoughtful way, and always called her "the ever-present daughter," considering I live miles away in another country, only visiting him briefly every few months when I could as my work keeps me busy in the middle east.

Lathamma in those 4 years served him beyond the call of duty. She stayed when the doctor visited. She monitored his medication along with the help of a male nurse and literally took over his diet. This enabled me to work where I am and earn enough to also provide for my father's care. Private medical services would have cost much more, but because Lathamma offered her help, I was able to provide the best medical care in the comfort of my home in India.

You may think, well, she was paid her housekeeper's Salary. That would lessen the value of her selfless service. It's the "no expectations" of loving service to my Dad like a family member beyond her regular duty hours, which I am grateful for. It was simple, pure kindness.

At the time of his death, "the ever-present daughter," Lathamma, was right there when he took his last breath, prayed for his soul, and genuinely wept at the loss of her adopted Dad. I, the "actual daughter," was in an airport waiting to board the flight to India when Daddy died. My loss for not being there to say goodbye, but

Lathamma represented me as the daughter who was miles away. I am grateful he didn't die alone but in the presence of a wonderful human being, Lathamma.

This little piece is to pay homage to my wonderful, loving, and generous Dad. But it is also my written tribute of eternal gratitude to Lathamma, "my soul sister." She is and will always remain my sister from another mother. May she always be blessed with joy and serenity in life.

"You may never know what results come of your actions. But if you do nothing, there will be no result."

— Mahatma Gandhi

97

A Smile, Camaro, and a Dollar of Grace

It was more than twenty years ago, but I remember it like yesterday. I had just left my boyfriend's house—tired, ready to be home—driving my beat-up Ford Escort down a familiar stretch of road.

I passed a Camaro. The driver glanced over—he was nice-looking—and we exchanged a quick, harmless smile. It was just one of those passing moments that usually disappear as fast as they come.

But a few minutes later, my car began to sputter. I tapped the gas pedal, hoping it was just a hiccup.

It wasn't. I'd miscalculated—I was out of gas.

I coasted to the shoulder. This was before cell phones. I had no way to call my sister, no money, and no idea what to do.

Then, headlights pulled up behind me. It was the Camaro.

The same guy stepped out—same smile, same calm presence. Without hesitation, he offered to help. He pushed my car all the way to the nearest gas station.

When we got there, I was trying to figure out how to call someone and how to get home. And then I looked down.

There, lying at my feet, was a crumpled dollar bill.

I never got his name. I never saw him again. But in that moment—stranded, broke, and alone—I felt something more than coincidence.

I felt God's quiet reassurance in the kindness of a stranger and a dollar that seemed to come from nowhere.

Some might call it luck. I call it grace.

"There is no such thing as chance or coincidence. Every moment of your life is guided by a greater wisdom."

— White Eagle

98

Clouds and Country Songs

This morning began with clouds.

I had a doctor's appointment for knee injections—the pain has made it hard to move around lately.

While the doctor worked, I closed my eyes and tried to meditate. To my surprise, the clouds I'd watched earlier returned—drifting behind my eyelids like a quiet promise.

Afterward, my husband and I stopped for lunch. On the way out, a Josh Turner country song was playing.

But as we walked to the car, I felt as if Jesus were gently asking me:

Would you go with me if we rode the clouds together?

Could you not look down forever,

If you were lighter than a feather?

Oh, and if I set you free... would you go with Me?

The lyrics touched something deep in me and brought tears to my eyes.

And right there, in the parking lot, I whispered, "Yes, I will go with you."

Sometimes, God doesn't speak through thunder or scripture—

but through clouds, knees, and yes... even country songs.

Nothing is too ordinary for God to use.

"If only you could see how close God is to you always—not far off in the heavens, but quietly shining in the smallest moments of your life."

— White Eagle

99

Navigating the Journey: A Life of Resilience

Growing up wasn't easy. School was a struggle—I didn't learn to read until first grade. Thankfully, my teacher that year was a loving and caring woman who believed in me.

Before that, Carol had been our family's nanny when I was around four, five, and six. After we moved, Kathy began helping take care of us. She was kind and dependable. Kathy frequently would stay the night. I especially loved when she made tuna fish sandwiches—there was something comforting about her presence.

My mother was beautiful and kind, but she struggled. She battled chemical dependency, and though I never knew exactly when it began, it left its mark on our family. In 1992, she went to a well-known treatment center for help. I still remember visiting for Family Week. I got to stay the night with her in her room and play basketball together—it was one of the last times we shared simple joy.

She came home for a short visit, and although I don't recall the details, I remember it felt hopeful. But not long after, my parents divorced. I remember the phone call when Mom told me. It felt like the ground gave way beneath me.

Eventually, my dad got custody. Life changed overnight. Mom moved into an apartment nearby and later, I believe, went to a halfway house. My aunt came to live with us to help take care of things. For a while, I wasn't allowed to ride in the car with Mom. I didn't understand it all—but I missed her terribly.

One day, I came home from school and was supposed to go to a church meeting. I walked in and found my dad and Mom's best friend sitting there. Dad's eyes were red. I couldn't figure out why her friend was there—until Dad blocked me from leaving. I realize now it was his way of protecting me. A few minutes later, he told me: my mother had passed away.

I was shattered. I didn't get to say goodbye.

In 1996, I was in a serious car accident—I was broadsided and spent over two weeks in the hospital. My spleen was removed, and for a while, I couldn't speak. Recovery was hard. I missed my prom. I turned around twice, trying to visit my mother's grave, but I just couldn't do it.

Eventually, I tried college and then came home. I moved around a bit, and had my daughter in 2005, and my son in 2008. Both births came with complications, but we got through it. Life wasn't easy, but there was joy too.

After years of working, I went back to school and earned my associate's degree. I've had surgeries since then, including a hysterectomy. I've lived with different people, made hard choices, and carried many regrets.

My relationship with my daughter has had its ups and downs, but she tells me she's forgiven me. That means the world to me. I hope, in time, others in the family might offer forgiveness, too.

I deeply love my two marvelous sisters—being able to talk with them, laugh, and share memories is a blessing I don't take for granted.

There were good times. Christmas at my grandmother's house was magical. So were the Christmases in our own home growing up—red bows everywhere, joy wrapped in ribbons and light. I remember those moments and hold them close.

I know my parents loved me the best they could. I wish I had felt it more clearly back then. I still miss my mother. I bring her flowers and visit her grave in our family plot. Sometimes, I think I can still hear her voice—beautiful, strong, full of song. My mom was a caring and thoughtful woman. She had this amazing singing voice I'll never forget. Even though things were hard, I know she loved me the best way she could. So did my dad. Everyone in my life—my sisters, my kids, the people who helped raise me, the ones who came and went—they've all touched my life in different ways. Each one, in their own way, helped shape who I am today. Sometimes, it's hard to make sense of it all, but I believe God's been with me through it. I think He's holding all of it—every person, every memory—in His hands. And somehow, God's helping me walk through my past so I can keep moving forward.

"When you pass through the waters, I will be with you; and when you pass through the rivers, they will not sweep over you."

— Isaiah 43:2

100

The Stillness That Held Me

While studying to become an ordained interfaith minister, I began working with a monk at a small temple in Arlington. He had started a weekly meditation group, and I found myself returning again and again, drawn by something I couldn't yet name. My meditation practice, however, was scattered—chaotic, really. Quieting the mind felt like trying to calm a storm with whispers.

Still, I kept showing up.

Over time, I attended retreats in Hawaii and closer to home. Then came an invitation that changed everything: a six-week immersion in the mountains of Chiang Mai, Thailand.

Eighteen of us gathered there, from all over the world. I was the only American. We didn't share a common language, yet somehow, we understood one another. I believe the meditation helped with that. Silence, it turns out, can be a bridge.

Each day began at 4 a.m. with two hours of meditation. Then we prepared food for the monks, shared our own simple breakfast, and spent the day rotating between chores and four more meditation sessions. They took everything from us—phones, devices, even our suitcases. We learned to live with only the most basic essentials. And surprisingly, that made space for something else to enter.

During the final week, we were invited to sit and meditate for as long as we could. I surprised myself: I sat for six hours straight. Others went even longer. But it wasn't about comparison. It was about presence. About stillness. About letting go.

That experience remains with me. Meditation is now woven into my life as a sacred tool. I lean on it in moments when I think I might not make it. And I return to it in moments when I am at peace, simply to remember.

In the quiet, I met God.

In the discipline, I found grace.

And in the stillness, I found my way back to myself.

"Don't you know yet?

It is your Light that lights the worlds."

— Rumi

101

The Sacred Heart

In my younger years, I did a lot of traveling for work. I was part of a marketing team for a medical software company, and my job included giving presentations, training staff, and manning booths at conferences. With an expense account in hand, I wined and dined potential clients and gave sales pitches over lavish meals. I was ambitious and committed, and I had my eyes on a big promotion. One contract in particular was highly coveted, and my company made it clear: if I secured it, the promotion would be mine.

One evening, after dinner with two executives—a CEO and a CFO from a major corporation—they made their offer clear: if I "showed them both a good time," they would guarantee the contract. If I didn't, they hinted that things could be made... uncomfortable. One of them leaned in and whispered, "If you do it in the next few hours, we can make things very sweet for you."

After paying the bill and leaving the restaurant, I felt nauseated. My heels were hurting, so I slipped them off and walked barefoot toward my hotel. I needed time to think.On the way, I passed a church just as a service was letting out. It was Ash Wednesday. I wasn't religious and never went to church, but something drew me in. The church was nearly empty, lit softly by flickering votive candles. I slipped into a pew at the back; the scent of candle wax hung in the air. I lit a candle and whispered to whoever might be listening, "What should I do?" As tears welled up and fell down my face, a deep peace settled over me

As I turned to leave, I noticed a statue of Jesus near the side exit. He stood with one hand pointing to a bright red heart at the center of His chest. In that quiet, sacred moment, I heard these words: *Follow your heart.*

Back at the hotel, I reached for the phone to call my supervisor—but before I could dial, she was calling me. I told her everything. To my relief, she was completely supportive. We didn't get the contract, and that was okay. With the help of my company, I filed a formal complaint against both executives. A couple of weeks later, I received a written apology from them for their unethical behavior.

But what has stayed with me far more than the apology or the lost account was that moment in the church—the clarity, the peace, the stillness.

"Nothing real can be threatened. Nothing unreal exists.
Herein lies the peace of God."

— *A Course in Miracles*

102

Never Broken

I knew limitations and problems in my life were caused by traumatic past events. I tried hard to heal from these traumas so I could live a happier life. To this end, I tried many healing workshops such as 'Healing the Inner Child,' 'Anger Releasing,' Reiki self-healing, EFT, and also more traditional approaches. All of these approaches correctly agreed that traumatic past events were causing me problems, and I needed to release beliefs built up around those memories. I experienced some wonderful healing moments through doing this, but somehow the effect always seemed to be temporary.

Then, one day, I found myself having a conversation with a friend who is a facilitator for the 3 principles. She pointed out to me that all my past traumas do not exist now. They exist as memory only. Please take a breath now and take a moment to let go of what you think you know about life. I ask you to do this so you can open to the possibility of seeing something new, something beautiful.

My friend then went further to explain that memories come to us via thought. When we are aware of our thoughts, we can drop them. Those past experiences do not exist anymore. That is because the only moment that exists is NOW. Yes, they were real when they happened. But now, they exist only as a memory. When you really think about it, of course, the only moment that exists is now.

Any perception of time beyond NOW is brought to us via thought. This allows us to perceive our life and the passage of time. And that is God's will. The sun appears to cross the sky, and very convincingly.

Yet we know it is the Earth moving around the Sun, making it seem that the Sun is moving, and the idea that the Sun crosses the sky is actually an illusion.

In the same way, our past experiences appear to exist, but in fact, they do not. In the same way, the passage of time is not real, but the power of thought makes it appear to be. The truth is NOW. When this is seen, we become free of the past. It evaporates like mist upon the ocean. And we are then free to live in the NOW. Free from illusory limitations, we uncover a world of unlimited possibilities. We find there was never anything to heal. We were already whole.

Our trauma was a dream, just a bad dream. And now we are awake in the reality of God, the reality of LOVE. We find we cannot unsee what we have seen. So we continue on our journey of forgetting and then remembering again, always drawing closer and closer to the one truth behind all truths. The truth of God.

"He heals the brokenhearted and binds up their wounds."

— Psalm 147:3

103

A Chain Reaction

It was my second year of college. I was working early mornings at a drive-through coffee shop. They open at 5:00 a.m. every morning. My work started at 4:30, where I made coffee and put out pastries. I worked this shift so I could get to my first class by 10:00.

A couple of months ago, the first customer, a woman in a red SUV, pulled up, paid for her drink, and handed me a twenty. "Use this for the person behind me," she said, almost like a secret.

I expected it to stop there—but it didn't. The man in the truck behind her laughed when I told him. "Well, shoot," he said, "guess I'll keep it going." He paid for the next car, and so did the next. It kept going, a chain reaction.

One woman added a croissant to her order for the person behind her. Then there was the man in the little silver sedan. He looked at the bumper stickers on the SUV ahead of him—plastered with strong political opinions—and raised his eyebrows. "Huh," he said, "I wonder if he'd still have bought my coffee if he knew who I voted for. He smiled. "It doesn't matter, does it? He did it. That's the thing."

As I watched this remarkable scene unfold, each order I filled gave me an unexpected boost of energy. People who looked rushed or frustrated began to smile when they learned about the chain. This continued for several hours, and not a single person broke the cycle until the last car pulled through. The entire vibe of the coffee house transformed.

Waking up before dawn still had its challenges, but it didn't feel as heavy anymore. There was something sacred about that line of headlights and hands reaching out for both coffee and connection. I even started keeping a couple of extra dollars in my apron pocket, just in case I wanted to be the first spark in another chain.

> "To give and to receive are one in truth."
>
> — A Course in Miracles

104

Journey of Fasting and Faith

On the second day of an apple fast, I received visions during my morning communion.

There is something miraculous about how freeing the body from digestion—or even the decision of what to eat—creates space for deeper clarity. I've come to believe that fasting is a sacred discipline I'll continue in some form, as I move more intentionally into a closer, daily walk with God.

I often hear from Jesus and Mother Mary during these quiet spaces, but this particular morning brought a rare visit from Mary Magdalene.

It happened in that thin space I call the *in-between time*, when resistance has been gently overruled by love and devotion.

I had asked the Holy Spirit to guide my fast and show me what I most needed to see. Immediately, Jesus appeared in a vision, gently pinning down my hand—as if to stop me from fleeing.

I dropped to my knees, head bowed in shame.

"Don't run, little one," he said. "I'll help you look deeper. I am here with you. I'll be here always. I am here with you forever."

Then I was carried into a different dimension, traveling through time on what felt like a celestial song. I asked again, "What is it I need to see?"

Suddenly, I saw it: the creation of many universes—bursting into being—then dissolving and reforming, like neurons lighting up across the sky of my mind. I received this knowing deep within: *Anything and everything can be created in God.*

Then Mother Mary appeared, radiant and steady. "Think thoughts of separation, and that is what you will have," she said. "Think only love from your heart, my dear child—for that is the better choice. Direct your heart in the direction of my heart, and recognize the divine genes you have inherited from your heavenly Creator."

When her voice quieted, Jesus returned. "No more running," he said. "Turn and face the staircase of your ascension." He held my hand and gently lifted my face. "Come now, and we shall climb this stairway of heaven together."

And then, something extraordinary happened. I felt Mary Magdalene's presence descend into me. It was as if her over-soul merged with mine, and suddenly I was both watching and experiencing her interaction with Jesus.

Still on my knees, I (and she) said: "I am not worthy to look into your face." Jesus lifted my chin again and said, "Look up, my child. You are *my* salvation. Your open heart and humble mind prepare me— strengthen me—to undergo the stations of the cross, which will be revealed as illusion through my resurrection. You, too, are a lamb, protected by the love of your Shepherd. You are worthy. You are my holy child, my friend, my companion—and even my savior, when you see your holy reflection through the dew drops of your tears. That reflection shines like a diamond in my sea of love, in my sky of magnificence. You are that reflection of magnificent beauty."

I have no better words to offer—only this blessing:

Deep peace, dear brothers and sisters.

May this story enter your soul as remembrance—of our Magnificence.

"You are altogether beautiful, my darling; there is no flaw in you."

— Song of Songs 4:7

105

A Sacred Task

I was always closely familiar with Jesus, starting in Sunday School in the Greek Orthodox Church. When I got older and the priests would say, "When Jesus went to study with the wise ones in his lost years," but never finished explaining, I always questioned—*Where did Jesus go? What did he study?* That was *exactly* what I wanted to know, yet I could never get a solid answer.

In my twenties, I began exploring. Yoga classes and regular massages opened something in me—my intuition, my questions, my curiosity about reincarnation. One night, I sat in bed praying to God, asking if reincarnation was real. A heavy guilt weighed on me. My religious upbringing was completely against such thoughts.

As I drifted off to sleep, I smelled roses near my left shoulder. Turning toward the scent, I felt Jesus' presence and heard Him gently say, "It's ok, it's all ok." Peace washed over me like a tide, and I fell asleep knowing my walk with Jesus had shifted—from reverent distance to tender, trusting friendship, like that of a beloved older brother.

Since that night, I've had many sacred encounters with Jesus and Mother Mary. I rarely speak of them, afraid of sounding boastful or unbelievable—but this one, I must share.

About ten years ago, I began praying face-down on my yoga mat, forehead to the floor. That posture—humble and grounded—seemed to open a deeper stillness. In a moment of breath and surrender,

Mother Mary appeared to me in a vision. She said, "Pray. Pray for the women, for women will change the world."

I answered from the center of my being, "Of course I will, Mary. I'll do that for you."

She showed me women of many cultures, each wearing scarves of various colors around their heads. I knew, then, she had given me a sacred task—to hold space for the divine feminine to rise, to serve God, and to help change the world.

As I slowly stood to begin the day, Jesus appeared in His light body. I blinked, thinking it was my imagination—but He remained. I closed my eyes halfway, unsure, and He said, "Go ahead. Touch my shoulder."

When I lifted my hand to His left shoulder, I felt the cool density of His etheric presence, like mist. He said, "Now touch the other," and as I did, the energy surged through me so powerfully I nearly fell backward. He caught me, steadying me with love.

Breathless, shaken, I dropped to my knees. The tears came—not from fear, but from awe. Overwhelming awe.

That moment remains one of the most sacred of my life. And now, I offer this: may you feel the transmission in your soul. May you pray for the rising of the divine feminine—not as division, but as healing. That we might all rise—together, shoulder to shoulder—in joy, in justice, in God's love.

"In the last days, God says, I will pour out my Spirit on all people.

Your sons and daughters will prophesy, your young men will see visions, your old men will dream dreams."

— Acts 2:17

106

Black Cat's Blessing: The Paws that Saved Me

One day, I was on my way to work. I always took a side road that was kind of a shortcut. There was a creek, and the road went straight down, and it had a 90-degree turn. Then you would go over a bridge and continue until you connected with another road.

There was a small farm with a barn right on the corner. I knew there was a turn to go over the bridge, but you couldn't really see the sign because the barn was in the way. On that day, a black cat appeared in the middle of the road, and it just sat there. I had been on that road every day for a year and had never seen any animals anywhere near that farm.

The cat was staring at me and kept looking up the road. He wouldn't budge, and I had to come to a complete stop, and I thought, "This is really strange." Within 15 seconds of stopping, this car barreled across that bridge and around that corner so fast he was in my lane. He almost lost it when he saw me, but fortunately, I was back up the road a little bit. As soon as the car came across, the black cat went into the barn. I was shaking, and when I got to work, I had to sit down. My co-workers asked if I was ok, and I told them I was saved by a black cat. There was no doubt in my mind that if that cat hadn't been there in that moment, I wouldn't be here today.

According to WikiHow, in many parts of the world, a black cat crossing your path is considered a sign that a guardian angel is protecting you or sending you good fortune.

I continued to drive to work on the same road for years, always looking, but my miracle cat was never seen again! That day, I felt that the cat had to have been my guardian angel, knowing that I would stop the car and wait for the kitty to move.

"The whole universe is conspiring to help you."

— Paulo Coelho

107

A Taste of Heaven

It was the summer of last year when the pain first arrived—sharp, unexpected, and mysterious. It settled deep in my stomach, persistent and unnerving. I brushed it off at first, convinced it would pass. I was 55, healthy, conscious of my diet, and in tune with my body. I had always taken good care of myself. But after four agonizing days, something told me this wasn't going away on its own. I finally went to the emergency room.

The diagnosis hit me sideways: acute pancreatitis. I blinked at the doctor, disbelieving. It didn't make sense. No history, no lifestyle markers, no logical reason. Just pain—and now, fear. What followed was a downward spiral: hospital stays, endless testing, weight loss, and, worst of all, the slow erosion of my spirit.

Over the course of the next three months, I lost 60 pounds. The person staring back at me in the mirror was barely recognizable—skin and bones, hollow eyes, a shadow of the vibrant man I once was. I had no strength, no appetite, and no will. I felt disconnected from everything that mattered: my joy, my music, my faith, even my reason for being. The light inside me was fading.

Doctors spoke in clinical tones: "pseudocysts," "malnutrition," "refeeding syndrome." I was on the brink of being put on a feeding tube. The prognosis was grim. I couldn't eat, not from lack of trying —but because my body simply wouldn't allow it. Every attempt brought pain, pressure, and disappointment.

Spiritually, I felt lost. Prayers felt empty. I was surrounded by hospital walls and machines, not peace or clarity. I began to prepare for the possibility that this was it—that my journey was coming to a close.

But then, something happened.

They handed me a nutrition shake—just a generic, off-brand hospital product. Nestlé, maybe. The day before, the very idea would have made me sick. But for reasons I still can't explain, I took a sip. And then another.

With each swallow, something extraordinary began to awaken in me—not just physically, but spiritually. I felt energy, warmth, and presence return to my body. It was as if God Himself was filling me, sip by sip, with life again. I could feel my heart space opening. Gratitude rushed in like a flood. I hadn't felt that connection to Spirit in months.

Within days, I was eating again. Real food. Solid food. Joyful food. Pizza and Mexican food—things that would've sent doctors into a panic weeks earlier were now somehow healing me. My body wasn't rejecting it—it was welcoming it, devouring it with an almost holy hunger. And I got stronger. Every day, a little more. My muscles returned. My voice carried more life. My laughter came back.

It was a miracle.

And I don't use that word lightly. This was a divine turning point. The prayers of so many—my friends, my community in Sedona, fellow healers, musicians, seekers—all those prayers had landed. I had spent decades giving: as a sound healer, astrologer, and musician. But now, I was receiving. All that love came back around. The circle is completed.

God hadn't abandoned me. He was simply waiting for the moment to pour grace into a space that had been emptied of everything else. When I had let go of all control, when my ego had been stripped bare, He arrived with abundance—not just of food, but of spirit, purpose, and love.

I share this story not to dwell on the suffering but to affirm the truth that miracles are real. That surrender can be sacred. And that sometimes, the most divine moments begin with something as simple as a sip from a plastic hospital cup.

Don't give up. Your miracle may be one breath, one prayer, or one sip away.

"For He satisfies the thirsty and fills the hungry with good things."

— Psalm 107:9

108

Pawprints of Heaven: The Music Returns

The silence in my house was unbearable. No sound of paws on the floor. No quiet breathing beside me. No one to say prayers with at night. Baxter was gone. After twenty-one years, my little white Pekingese — my companion, my anchor, my heart — was gone. He had seen me through it all. The heartbreak of divorce, the lonely nights after the spotlight faded, the moments I wasn't sure I wanted to keep going. He stayed. He loved. He healed me in ways no one else could. And when he left, something inside me broke.

I didn't want another dog. Not really. Friends kept suggesting it, trying to help, but nothing felt right. No face, no tail, no wagging body came close to touching what I had lost. Then, out of nowhere, a friend — a concert pianist like me — reached out from Rhode Island. She said she had a present for me. A little something to lift my spirits. I thought maybe it was flowers. Maybe chocolates. Maybe something thoughtful but simple. What she didn't tell me — what I wouldn't find out until later — was that she had been searching. That she had felt Baxter, somehow, guiding her. And that he had led her to a tiny town in Texas, called Sulpher Springs, just miles from my hometown of Fort Worth. Of all the places in the world, this pup had been waiting near the place where my own story began.

When the doorbell rang, I opened it, hesitant — still heavy from the grief I carried. And there he was. Not my friend from Rhode Island, but the delivery man. Holding out a soft blue blanket wrapped around something warm and trembling. I pulled the blanket back... And there he was. A white Pekingese puppy blinked up at me with a calm I recognized in my bones. The breath left my body. My knees gave out. And I wept — loud, guttural sobs that had waited weeks to break free. Because this wasn't just any dog; this was Baxter's gift. His message. His handoff.

This was Easton. From the moment he entered my home, he knew. He found Baxter's toys. He walked to the food dish without being shown. And that night —God as my witness — when I knelt to pray, Easton placed one paw on each of my shoulders, just like Baxter used to do. You can call it a coincidence. You can call it magic. I call it love. The kind that never leaves. The kind that waits for the right time, in the right form, to come back and carry you forward. That day, with a blue blanket in my arms and tears streaming down my face, I met Hope again. I felt joy again. I heard it — soft at first but clear. The music came back.

"Until one has loved an animal, a part of one's soul remains unawakened."

— Anatole France

109

Her Last Supper and Prayer of Love

A few years ago, my dear friend was in the final stages of her long battle with breast cancer. I went to visit her in the hospital, and when I walked into the room, I saw her uncle and her mother quietly sitting by her side.

I wanted so badly to pray over her. I could feel the pull in my heart—but I was nervous. Her supper arrived, so I offered to feed her some of the fruit from the tray. She was so weak I wasn't sure she'd be able to eat, but she managed a few small bites. I sat there beside her, offering what I could.

When she had finished, I got up to chat with her uncle and her mom, still wrestling with whether to ask if we could pray together. I hesitated, unsure of how they'd respond. Eventually, I drifted toward the end of the room, leaning against the doorframe—still undecided, still questioning.

And then, it happened.

I felt a distinct, undeniable poke in my side. It was firm, like someone nudging me with urgency. I spun around, but no one was there. My heart knew instantly: this was Spirit. Spirit saying, *Yes! Go now. Do this!*

With courage that came from somewhere beyond me, I walked back to my friend's bedside. I invited her mother and uncle to join hands with me, and we stood together, praying for her peace, comfort, and safe passage. Love filled the room like light.

The next day, she passed.

At her funeral, I stood in the receiving line, heart heavy but full of gratitude. When I reached her husband, he looked directly into my eyes, gently took my shoulders, and said, *"You fed her her last supper."*

Time stopped. My heart cracked wide open.

I hadn't known. I hadn't planned. But somehow, I had been given the holy honor of serving love in its purest form. It remains one of the most sacred moments of my life—a small act that became a miracle.

"Christ has no body now but yours, no hands, no feet on earth but yours..."

— St. Teresa of Avila

110

Change Left Behind

It happened at the Brookshire's in Bowie, Texas. I was third—or maybe fourth—in line when I noticed something unusual at the register. A man had just paid for his groceries and left an extra $10 for the person behind him.

But that person declined.

So did the next one.

And then it was my turn. I, too, passed on the gift—not out of unkindness, but because I felt it should go to someone who truly needed it.

The cashier smiled, shook his head gently, and said, "I wonder if I'll still have this extra ten dollars by the end of my shift."

There was something touching in his voice—not quite disbelief, but quiet awe. Because even if no one had accepted the money yet, someone had chosen to give. And that simple act was enough to shift the energy in the room.

It reminded me: yes, there are still a lot of good people in the world. Sometimes, all it takes is ten dollars—and the heart behind it—to remind us.

"Give, and it will be given to you. A good measure, pressed down, shaken together and running over, will be poured into your lap."

— Luke 6:38

111

A Grieving Heart

I used to be the one who packed fruit cups and hummus, cut strawberries into hearts, and lined up little cheese cubes on pretzel sticks. Everyone had a nutritious meal for dinner. I used to have everyone's laundry clean and folded with clothes laid out for the children in the morning. I used to play outside with the children, limiting TV and time spent on their devices. I was the perfect mother and wife.

That was before leukemia visited Jeremy, my husband. Little by little, it took every bit of life from my partner and best friend. But it took me along with him, only leaving a shell behind.

Now, the kids get peanut butter and jelly sandwiches and a cookie. Fast food is for dinner more times than not. Now the laundry basket is overflowing, and I am searching for clean socks, and who cares if they match? Now, the kids watch as much TV as they want.

The house is a wreck, and I can barely get out of bed in the mornings.

Then I see my mother-in-law's car park in the driveway. Oh, Hell No! She didn't call; she just showed up. Just what I don't need! The house is in need of a good cleaning; the kids and I are a mess. My eyes were still bloodshot from crying. We had always gotten along, but that was before Leukemia took away my beloved. I opened the door. She's been crying too. After all, she lost her firstborn. I make an excuse for the way the house looks, with a pile of laundry, the kids' toys, and school supplies.

She said I didn't come to see your house, I came to see you. I confided that since Jeremy died, I have become a horrible mother. It was all I could do to make sure the kids had something to eat and clean socks. She told me that it was a struggle for her, also. Yet she assured me that I was doing the best I could. The children have food to eat, and they have clean clothes. They have just lost their father, and TV and their devices are a comfort while they grieve. That is not being a horrible mother; it's being gentle and allowing everyone time to heal.

She wrapped her arms around me in a hug. We both sobbed -deep, shaking sobs as we held each other. While we shared our grief in that embrace, I felt something holy was holding us together. This was over 7 years ago. We still miss Jeremy, but that "holy presence" still holds us together.

> "Blessed are those who mourn, for they shall be comforted."
>
> — Matthew 5:4

112

The Gifts She Taught Me

My grandmother survived the Holocaust, but she never let it harden her heart. Instead, she became a collector of what my mother called "quiet wonders." She would tell me that every day God hands you gifts. Most aren't wrapped paper or tied with a bow—but they're there. As a child, I didn't always understand, but she would point them out: a soft breeze, the smell of the air after a rain, a stranger's smile, a kind word at just the right moment.

She taught me that some gifts come dressed as disappointments. Like when my first boyfriend broke my heart, and I thought the world had ended. "This too, is a gift," Grandma said gently. Years later, I'd see the truth in that—how that heartbreak carved out space for the love that was meant for me.

But it wasn't just about receiving. "We must gift the world, too," she'd remind me. "Not just on birthdays or holidays—but every day." Feed a stray cat. Pick up a bit of trash. Leave water out for the birds. Call someone who might be lonely. Smile, even if you don't feel like it. These are the gifts that matter most.

Now, when I take my morning walk and pause to admire a bloom or greet a neighbor, I hear his voice in the wind saying, "Life itself is the gift. The rest is how we wrap it."

"Whoever saves a life, it is considered as if he saved an entire world."

— from the Talmud, Tractate Sanhedrin 4:9

113

Love Is the Oldest Magic

We were still in our robes, driving home from a solstice gathering in the hills—muddy, tired, and in need of hot showers. Thom was humming a chant under his breath, the kind that gets in your bones and settles there.

I spotted the car before he did—a white SUV pulled off on the shoulder, hazard lights blinking. A man with a cast on his leg leaned against the door, and a very pregnant woman stood beside him. They were trying to jack up the vehicle, but weren't getting far.

"Pull over," I said. We parked behind them and turned on our flashers. Their bumper was covered in religious and stickers—crosses, Bible verses, *What Would Jesus Do?*

I felt a bit of hesitation. I've had people look at me sideways for wearing a pentacle, for calling myself a witch, for saying *blessed be* instead of *God bless*. But mercy is mercy. And when someone's stranded with a swollen belly, that's not the time to worry about religion or politics.

Thom got down on the ground and started working on the tire. I walked over with a couple of water bottles and handed them to the couple. They took them like they were holy.

The woman glanced at the crystals around my neck. "We were just coming back from a solstice gathering," I offered gently.

She looked curious but only said, "Oh."

When the tire was fixed, the man tried to give us money. Thom smiled and shook his head.

"It's just good to help," he said. "It's what we believe. And it would be what Jesus would do."

We all chuckled.

I'll never forget the way she looked at me—as if something had shifted. She teared up a little and gave me a hug. Thom and the man shook hands. It was if we weren't so different after all. That day, we didn't just change a tire. We bridged something.

Love is really the oldest magic.

"Love and compassion are necessities, not luxuries.
Without them humanity cannot survive."

— Dalai Lama

114

His Steadfast Love

Walking in faith is a journey, not a destination.

February and March 2025 have been months of celebration—marking a full year of victories.

In March of last year, I was diagnosed with stage 4 lung adenocarcinoma and told I had just three months to live. But the Lord, in His mercy, led us to a specialist who delivered unexpected and hope-filled news: my molecular study revealed a rare lung cancer mutation called *EGFR*. Because of that mutation, I qualified for a targeted cancer therapy—a "miracle pill."

The doctor was elated, offering handshakes, hugs, and high-fives. Little did we know we were stepping into something even greater—a miraculous journey with the Lord. Yes, defeating cancer saved my body, but God had a deeper healing in store. One filled with His powerful, loving presence.

I have walked in the shadow of His mighty love. Every battle has been a victory, and today I stand whole—in body, mind, and spirit.

As of June 2025, I now celebrate three PET scans and MRIs showing no cancer and an echocardiogram that was called perfect. I never tire of hearing those miraculous words! I'm working on regaining strength and mobility, enjoying more independence, and continuing to live with the steadfast hope that has always carried me.

The statistics say I may have three years. But because I've responded so well to treatment—with no side effects—there is hope for many more years. Praise the Lord!

Why three years? This particular cancer is known to be sneaky—it can mutate again, potentially making current treatment ineffective. But thanks be to God, new targeted therapies are already in development, and one is said to be even better. I trust that God already has a plan in place if that time ever comes.

I am on God's timetable. This walk has been nothing short of miraculous. We've witnessed wonders—physical, emotional, and spiritual. Scripture tells me to believe in God's power to heal, and if I ever had any doubt, this past year erased it. His care, protection, and healing have come in endless ways.

As for our family, they are my champions. Their teamwork and faith surround me with strength and love, creating a world of possibilities. I'm covered in support and prayer—from friends nearby and far away, from our church and community, and even from strangers. Some encounters feel angelic. I truly believe heaven is hovering.

I am a blessed woman. In every part of my life, I experience mercy, kindness, patience, goodness, hope, faith, joy, peace—and above all, love.

"You make known to me the path of life; you will fill me with joy in your presence, with eternal pleasures at your right hand."

— Psalm 16:11

"I praise you because I am fearfully and wonderfully made; your works are wonderful, I know that full well."

— Psalm 139:14

115

Memories of Juneteenth

President Obama said today, "Even in the darkest hour, there is cause to hope for tomorrow's light." His words reminded me of a hot summer day when I saw that hope in a public park.

It was probably more than 25 years ago when I was a home health nurse working in some of the poorest neighborhoods in town. Many of my patients didn't have air conditioning. Most ran out of money days before their next Social Security check arrived. One of my patients had a dirt floor. But what they did have was grit and a kind of generosity of spirit.

I came to love those patients. Over time, they began to feel like extended family. I celebrated their recoveries, worked with social workers trying to get their medications paid, grieved their passing, attended funerals, and have many of their stories in my heart.

Every year, some of these families would gather for a Juneteenth picnic at a local park. And every year, several of my patients would invite me—"You gotta come this year."

One year after several persistent invitations, I promised to attend. I put the plate of chocolate chip cookies at the end of fried chicken, brisket, collard greens, potato salad, and watermelon. I was a little unsure as I was the only white person there. Yet, I was greeted with open arms. I arrived around 11:30 a.m. The park was already alive with music, laughter, lawn chairs, and kids playing. The celebration had started around 10 and would go well into the night.

For some reason, I didn't feel out of place. I saw familiar faces—people I had helped heal, people who had once let me into their homes and lives, told me their secrets, and let me hold their pain in my hands. The color of my skin didn't matter that day. What mattered was trust, care, and shared history.

I stayed just until about 1:00, but in that short time, I was hugged, fed, and made to feel like I belonged.

That day reminded me that healing happens when we show up, listen, and love across lines that history once used to divide us. One person at a time.

"Love is the only force capable of transforming an enemy into a friend."

— Dr. Martin Luther King, Jr

116

Hearts and Angels: A Celebration of Innocence

I work in early childhood development and education as a teacher. Currently, I have a large group of children ranging from 4 to 12 years of age. Most of the children are challenged or at risk in some way. When I began to work here a little while ago, I became acquainted with two sisters who have been in several foster homes and have been relegated to supervised visits with their one parent, who has had suicidal associations. These girls were often withdrawn, untrusting, and frequently sad.

Our center is a secular school, and topics are not discussed in relation to God, religion, etc., but we can certainly show love.

On that particular day, I was seated at a table with some other children, and the two sisters, along with two other girls, approached me very quietly and purposefully. They were beaming and glowing, and in a very ceremonious processional, they presented to me, all in unison, a large 3-dimensional multi-colored cross they had all constructed together very carefully out of "waffle blocks." The eldest of the sisters looked deeply into my eyes and said, "This is Jesus, and these 36 additional smaller crosses are angels." Then she opened up the "Jesus "cross, and in the middle was a smaller cross. She said, "And this is Jesus' heart."

In our quiet, timeless, Holy bubble, Jesus and His angels stepped in. I told them that Jesus is with them, and so are the angels, and how it is that I recognized them all as "sisters," which REALLY made them

BEAM!! Each of them acknowledged, nodded, and agreed very affirmatively in unison. Now, having completed their very important and holy task, they carefully and reverently carried the crosses away to sequester them in a safekeeping place somewhere in the room.

A few moments after that, I observed that another child, an older boy who might be characterized as the tough, testosterone 12-year-old boss leader of the "turf," who had been secretly and furtively watching all of this, was now himself, purposefully building an even bigger 3-dimensional cross out of something we have called "magnetic tiles". While he was building this, he was very quietly and shyly singing a song to himself that I have been teaching them, that before then, he wouldn't even begin to sing along with us, because of course, that wouldn't have been "cool"!

We were divinely blessed and unified in one holy moment. Yes, it was very BIG.

"Jesus said, 'Let the little children come to me, and do not hinder them, for the kingdom of heaven belongs to such as these.'"

— Matthew 19:14

117

The Blue Scarf

They moved me here about six months ago. I call it "here" because "home" just doesn't feel right anymore. My legs aren't as steady as they used to be, and I forget little things—names, dates, where I put my glasses. But the things that matter, I still remember. My husband's laugh and the hymn we sang at our wedding.

Most days are quiet. Meals come on time. The nurses are kind enough. But I feel invisible. The world has moved on without me.

Then, one day, a young woman came in—a volunteer, they said. A college student, bright-eyed and a little nervous, carrying a knitting bag. She sat next to me and said, "I'm Mia. I want to learn to knit. Would you teach me?"

My fingers hadn't knitted in years, but they still knew what to do. As I showed how to start and Mia was a quick learner. We met every week. I remembered the baby blankets, winter hats, gloves, and even a couple of sweaters I made.

As we knitted, we talked. I told her about my husband, who passed away in '94, and how he'd sing hymns off-key just to make me laugh. She told me about losing her mom when she was twelve and how some days still felt empty.

One afternoon, I shared something I'd never told anyone: "Sometimes I wonder why I'm still here. I don't feel like I'm much use anymore."

Mia looked up and said softly, "But you are. You're the only one who really listens. You remind me what kindness feels like."

In that moment, I knew God had heard me. I'd been praying to feel needed, to matter. And He answered—not with thunder or light, but with a girl and a ball of yarn.

Last week, she gave me a gift—a blue scarf. It was perfect. "I made it for you," she said, "because you helped me feel loved." I could have cried.

Some people wait for miracles. But sometimes, God comes wrapped in blue with a quiet voice that lets me know I am loved and still valuable.

"Even to your old age and gray hairs I am he, I am he who will sustain you. I have made you and I will carry you; I will sustain you and I will rescue you."

— Isaiah 46:4

118

Against All Odds

Melody and I grew up in the same town and attended the same schools. While we knew each other, we were in different social circles. She was raised in a home filled with music—her mother played the piano, and her dad played guitar and violin, which he always called a fiddle. Melody played both instruments and excelled in the school music program. She was even accepted into the Berklee College of Music. I was in advanced placement classes, inspired to become a physician.

It was the first day of our junior year of high school when everything shifted. Melody passed me in the hall, her long brown hair and her beautiful blue eyes. Then she looked at me and said, 'Hi!' At that moment, my world started to orbit around her. She stole my heart.

My grades never slipped, but she was always on my mind. My parents adored her. They even invited her to play at one of their parties. I became a regular fixture at her house—studying while she practiced her music, perfecting each piece. We were always together. She was my best friend.

When she performed onstage with her family, my parents often came to watch.

During the last semester of high school, our love deepened—and we let it express itself physically. We were both smart, but in that season of passion, the last thing we thought about was prevention.

Over spring break, Melody became ill. She started throwing up and blamed it on something she'd eaten. But a few days later, it dawned on her: she might be pregnant.

A home test confirmed it.

We sat in silence. We were at a crossroads, not sure which path to take. All I knew was that I loved her—and I wanted this baby. I thought I knew Melody inside and out, but in that moment, I realized I didn't know what she truly wanted. She would only say I can't tell you what to do.

We decided to tell our parents together. I didn't want her to face them alone.

We gathered both sets in her living room. Melody's dad was the first to speak, laying out the options. His first suggestion was abortion. At that, Melody instinctively placed a hand over her tummy as if protecting our unborn child. Tears welled in her eyes and spilled down her cheeks.

He gently reminded her that life could go on—she could still go to Berklee, and I could still pursue my education. Another option, he said, was to have the baby, and I could live as if this never happened—aside from the next eighteen years of child support. Or she could choose adoption.

Then he looked at us and said quietly, "I want you to understand—the odds are against your relationship surviving this. Most don't."

My dad spoke next. "Melody, we love you, and we'll support your decision. But honestly, we'd love to be able to hold our grandchild and watch them grow up."

Then I said, "There's another option."

I got down on one knee in front of our parents and Melody. "Marry me. Let's raise this child together. You are my best friend. I can't imagine life without you by my side."

After graduation, we were married in my parents' backyard.

Our beautiful baby girl, Harmony, was born a few months later. She has a small birthmark on her inner ankle—in the shape of a heart. Melody teases me. That's where my heart goes.

Melody is still my best friend, and she still has my heart.

This year, Harmony graduated from high school; her brother and sister are a few years behind. We have made it against all odds.

"Love bears all things, believes all things, hopes all things, endures all things   Love never fails."

— 1 Corinthians 13:7–8

119

Together in Light: The Collective Power of Consciousness

What we do inside can actually change the outside world!

One of the great truths of quantum physics is that the same force that created the whole universe is somehow connected with our own consciousness. In other words, what we do inside can actually connect and change the outside world in ways we never thought possible.

When I was growing up, at night, when I was asleep, I would sometimes have dreams that would come true at some later time in my waking life. I never knew when the dreams would come true, just that my life would happen exactly the way I had previously dreamed. In other words, I was aware that my dreams were predicting my life. I was still a kid, so I thought that everyone had these dreams. So I really never thought much about it and most certainly never told anybody about it.

As I grew up and went to college, I became increasingly curious about life and, in particular, whether there was a God or not. I couldn't understand how my dreams would predict things with such accuracy and where this information came from. So, I kind of had the idea that there was more to life than I could put my finger on.

In college, I decided to take a trip to India and the Far East so I could explore different religions. In particular, I was curious about what Buddhism and Hinduism had to say about God during this exploration. I got very sick and actually had a life-after-death experience. At the time, I knew nothing about this experience, but during the event, I was given information about what was happening. What I saw was that the universe vibrated and flowed in divine light and that all of humanity was composed of that same light. So, the main conclusion of this experience was that I realized that our consciousness was part of the same force that created this universe.

As a result, I decided to conduct scientific research to help prove that what we do inside can change the outside world. I entered Graduate School and came up with the idea that people who are meditating could possibly influence the outside world in beneficial ways. I figured if people got into a higher state of consciousness, then they might be able to impact the world more than they would normally. I thought that meditation would be a good thing to study and see if it had an influence on the outside world to kind of prove my hypothesis.

At that time, I knew there was a whole bunch of people who were doing Transcendental Meditation, and many of them had started at the same time. I figured I would look at the crime rates before and after this large group of people started meditation. We also looked at auto accidents and even suicides. I even compared them with cities that did not have large groups of meditators so that way I would have a good control group.

And what we found was amazing! Not only did crime rates decrease dramatically by 20 or 30%, but also auto accidents and even suicides were significantly reduced. Now, 35 years later, there are over 40 studies proving that we are indeed connected to the outside world. So, what we do inside can indeed change the outside world, especially when we get into higher states of consciousness.

In many ways, this is very similar to the prayer research, which also has found that we can connect and change the outside world. At this point, we've done over 40 significant studies, and the results are quite conclusive that we are indeed connected with those in our surrounding community. So, in essence, we are not alone but are connected in a very fundamental way with all of humanity.

But more important to me was the idea that when we raise our consciousness and expand our consciousness, then we can have a good effect on everyone around us. We are not helpless! With all this negative stuff going around us, we can make a difference by focusing on positive things. The research is conclusive that we can make the world a better place simply by expanding our own consciousness and changing ourselves.

"You are not a drop in the ocean. You are the entire ocean in a drop."

— Rumi

120

Miracles Happen: Our Story of Faith and Healing

In January, my family experienced something so painful it brought us to our knees—and showed us that miracles still happen.

On January 5th, my grandson Sabacito developed what seemed like a simple cough. The doctor diagnosed him with croup and sent him home with treatment. But that night, his breathing worsened, and my daughter and son-in-law rushed him back to the hospital.

The doctors quickly realized the standard treatment wasn't working. They explained that 97% of children respond well to it—but Sabacito fell into the 3% who do not. He was admitted to the ICU and placed on oxygen. Still, he didn't improve.

On January 7th, after further testing, doctors confirmed it was influenza croup. We watched helplessly as teams of specialists surrounded him, trying to determine the best path forward. As a family, we cried and prayed while his tiny body grew weaker.

Finally, the doctors made the decision to try heliox—a blend of helium and oxygen delivered through a large mask. The tanks were enormous and out of place in the ICU room, but they offered a glimmer of hope. Because his airways were so swollen, regular oxygen couldn't reach his lungs. The heliox, being lighter, could.

It was our last hope before intubation.

On January 13th, our prayers were answered. Sabacito improved enough to be taken off heliox and placed on regular oxygen. He was able to eat again. And on January 14th, he was released from the ICU.

Those days were some of the hardest of our lives. But the miracle came—not only through the treatment but through the unshakable power of prayer. Family and friends prayed day and night. Many candles were lit, and many rosaries were said. We witnessed the strength of our faith and were reminded that God was with us in that room, holding our grandson when we could not.

Miracles are real. We lived one.

"Faith does not make things easy, it makes them possible."

— Luke 1:37

121

Love Without Limits: The Veterinarian's Role

I grew up on a farm where everything depended on the weather. If the rain didn't come, neither did the money. My parents were hospitable people—too "people-y" for my taste, if I'm honest. I was a quiet kid, much happier with animals than with crowds. My best friends were my dog, Buster, and my cat, Mr. Meow. I knew early on that farming wasn't for me. Animals? Yes. People? Not so much.

That's how I decided to become a veterinarian. I figured I could spend my life caring for pets and avoiding most human interaction. Now that's a laugh.

It didn't take long after graduating to learn the truth: every pet comes with a person and sometimes a whole family, and they often need just as much care and attention—sometimes more. I've seen couples fight over pet custody during divorces. I've seen people more inconsolable over the loss of a pet than the death of a spouse. I've watched clients beam with pride when their dog finally learned to sit, as if it had just graduated from MIT.

Love knows no boundary, and it certainly doesn't stop at species. Some days were rough, like when we had to say goodbye to a beloved companion. We always sent sympathy cards, and I can't tell you how many times people reached out just to thank us for that small kindness. Other days were joyful, like when a client brought in a new puppy or kitten, full of hope and fresh beginnings. And there were always cookies—homemade chocolate chip cookies showing up at the front desk as a thank-you for healing not just their animal, but their heart.

I'd always thought of myself as an animal person. But somewhere along the way, without even trying, I became a people person too.

"Veterinarians may treat animals, but they also heal the hearts of those who love them."

— Unknown

122

What They Left Behind

Isn't it annoying when the only way to learn something is by going through the hard way—when a bit of knowledge ahead of time could've made all the difference?

When my father died unexpectedly—just six months after my mother—my brother and I suddenly found ourselves standing in a house we had visited dozens of times. We knew where the sticking plasters were, what was in the fridge, and where the spare duvet was. But we had no idea where they kept their personal papers or documents.

It became even more complicated because our parents had lived in France for the past twenty years. We had just ten days to organize a funeral and sort through all the essential details—utilities, banking, insurance—navigating it all in a foreign language.

We felt like burglars, rifling through drawers and files in a home that had always been a place of comfort. It was disorienting and deeply emotional.

And yet, in the middle of all that, we began to uncover small treasures: personal mementos, notes, and keepsakes. We found the first letter my eldest son had written to them. We found testimonials from people whose lives had been touched by Mum and Dad's kindness and generosity. These small discoveries were like hidden love letters they had left behind.

It was a long time before we even found their passports—something they barely needed anymore, living in the EU.

This experience made me determined to make things easier for my own family when my time comes. I want them to know where things are. I want to leave clarity—not confusion—behind.

So here's my message: Don't Wait!

Ask your parents. Share your stories. Let them tell you where the important things are—and what really mattered to them. Learn from my experience, and make space for these conversations before it's too late.

"Teach us to number our days, that we may gain a heart of wisdom."

— Psalm 90:12

123

Coming Home to God

This is My Miracle Story. There was a time in my life when I felt spiritually adrift. I was moving through a personal crisis that touched every layer of my being — emotional, physical, and soul-deep. I was still working as a holistic practitioner, fully present for those I supported, but something inside me was quietly unraveling. It was as if my spirit was calling out — not in despair, but in longing. I needed to come home to something I had forgotten.

Then, during a session, one I was giving, not receiving, something extraordinary happened. The atmosphere changed. A warm, luminous presence filled the space. I didn't see with my eyes, but with something deeper. I felt the essence of Jesus — not as a religious figure, but as pure, unconditional love. A knowing entered me, wordless but clear: You belong to Heaven. You are held.

That moment marked the beginning of a deep inner awakening. In another session, a sacred memory stirred within me — something ancient, feminine, and filled with light. Though I couldn't explain it fully, it felt connected to the Divine Mother, a lineage of love I somehow knew. Not as dogma or belief, but as soul-truth.

Shortly afterward, I came across a video by Michael Mirdad on Christ. His words felt like medicine for my spirit. Listening to him, I remembered something I'd never truly forgotten — the language of my soul. Through his work, I encountered the message of the Daughter of Heaven. The moment I heard those words, I knew they belonged to me. Not as a title, but as a recognition. A return.

From then on, my life began to change. I found a spiritual family, a deep sense of belonging, and a renewed connection to God — one that transcended religion and awakened pure truth, trust, and love. I now live in quiet connection, walking with Spirit, guided by something greater and more intimate than I had ever known.

This was the miracle: not a single moment, but a series of soul-remembrances that brought me back to who I truly am. And for that, I am endlessly grateful.

"You do not need to seek love, only to remove the barriers you have built against it."

— A Course in Miracles

124

The Search

There was a time in my life when I had lost touch with any sense of Spirit in the world. Through most of my teens and twenties, I was an avowed atheist. I felt no particular need to search for anything deeper. Looking back, I would now call that season "the dark night of my soul." I was full of doubt, clinging to a sort of rugged individualism and a proud skepticism that insisted I didn't need anything outside of myself. But sometime in my mid-thirties, something shifted. I began to feel a longing for more—a sense of purpose, a connection I realized had been missing. Raised in the Catholic faith, I naturally began my search there, revisiting the roots of what I had been taught. Figuratively—and literally—I started searching for God.

I began walking the woods around my childhood hometown. I didn't know exactly what I was looking for at first, only that I was looking for something. Eventually, I realized I was seeking God. I wanted answers. I wanted to know my role in this life. At some level, without fully realizing it, I had begun to believe again. And now I wanted God to reveal Himself to me—maybe even like He had to Moses.

One day, while walking on Nobscot Hill in Sudbury, I was on my way back to the car, feeling discouraged. I hadn't found God the way I'd imagined. That's when I noticed a small tree with a curious loop in its trunk—growing upward, then bending in a complete circle before rising again. It struck me as both strange and beautiful.

As I stood there, everything became still. I was no longer in my head—I was fully present. I looked up at the sky, its brilliant blue, the white clouds drifting by. I closed my eyes and heard the wind, imagined it whispering to me. I opened my eyes again and saw the greenness of the trees more vividly than I ever had.

In that moment, understanding fell into place.

There was Life in everything. Spirit in everything. In me, in the sky, in the trees, and in the soil. The same Spirit that filled the world was part of me. I realized then that God—Great Spirit, as I now prefer—was not something separate who would appear before me. Spirit had always been here, all around and within. I had just been blind to the Presence.

We are all connected through Spirit, and Spirit is connected through us. A deep peace settled in me. I had finally opened my eyes to see what had always been there. By letting go of how I thought it should happen, I found exactly what I had been searching for.

"You were never searching alone. The One you seek has always walked beside you."

— Author unknown

125

Light Beyond the Rash

Eighty years ago, at age 2, I was diagnosed with Eczema (atopic dermatitis). Thus began a life of an itchy rash covering my body. I scratched and bled for the next 14 years. Half of my first-grade school year went by before I was well enough to attend.

My maternal Grandmother sewed little white long-sleeved jackets for me to wear to school. My first-grade teacher was empathetic. When I bled through my jacket sleeves, she gently said, "Bonnie Sue, it's time for you to go home." During the next decade, the Eczema spread over most of my body. Thankfully, my small-town classmates were kind and didn't ostracize me.

My eighth-grade basketball coach recruited me because I was tall. I told him I had two left feet. He said, "Bonniper Bishopper, you can do it". The Basketball uniforms exposed my wounds, and even knee pads failed to hide the open wounds behind my knees. Visiting crowds taunted me. I wanted no more of hearing people saying, "Oh, that girl has a rash...I hope my daughter doesn't touch her because she might be contagious". Our year was more than successful. But enough is enough, I reasoned.

High school found me still wearing long sleeves year-round. Then there was a day I'll never forget. In a school assembly, a girl whom I befriended when others didn't bravely stood and nominated me for cheerleader. Much to my surprise, I was elected! That was a lightbulb moment. Even though I was still battling my Eczema, I felt that God was giving me the courage and opportunity to be a light for others. I would not allow my disease to ruin my life. I would use it as an instrument of love to help others.

I recall an incident when I woke with huge scales covering my face and neck. Mom helped me peel the flakes of dead skin off to make me more presentable for a special school event. Some nights, Mom or Dad sat by my bedside holding my arms so that I could not scratch myself to the point of bleeding…the itching never stopped.

Over the years, my family doctor had always been searching for new treatments. Once he smeared black coal tar on my arms, then wrapped them from my armpit to my wrist in white gauze. I could not bend them for several days.

When Cortisone was created by one of my doctor's colleagues in Houston, we tried it, and for the first time in my life, I began to have normal-looking skin! In a year, I looked and felt like a different girl. I thanked God every night for His amazing gift!

There were times when I was a young person dealing with eczema that I thought," Why me?". But, in reality, I thought it shaped me into a more empathetic person. One of my passions for most of my life, and particularly today, is to help in any way I can people who are less fortunate in life.

"I will restore you to health and heal your wounds,"
declares the Lord."

— Jeremiah 30:17

126

Perfectly Imperfect

As a child, I always wanted to be perfect. When I would bring home a grade of 97 instead of 100, my dad would tell me that there was room for improvement. His voice wasn't harsh, but the message stuck. So I either tried to be perfect, or if the goal was too hard or unattainable, I wouldn't try.

Even after I had grown, I tried to be the perfect wife and mother.

If I am honest, to this day, when I want to impress someone, there is still a bit of the desire for perfection streak that lingers. Looking back, those instances didn't matter.

Many times, if I wanted to write a letter, I'd use scrap paper to practice. I'd write and rewrite until I was finally happy with how something looked or sounded. Then, I'd try to copy it onto the clean page. But often, it never looked quite as good. I'd press too hard or spell something wrong. And there it was—failure on that sacred, unmarred sheet.

I remember one day, I was driving home from work and just said, "Why can't I be perfect?"

A couple of days later, I went for a walk near a wooded area where I often found peace.

As I stood among the trees, I felt something: a quiet, holy presence. The Holy Spirit. Not loud, not booming. Just... present. The kind of stillness that asks you to listen. "Look at the trees," came the whisper.

I looked. Different varieties, some tall, some small, some with broken branches. Some with knots and twists in their trunks. All different. All alive.

Then came the question, quiet but clear: "Which tree is not perfect?"

I stood in silence on the verge of tears. They were all perfect. The Holy Spirit's message was gentle but unshakable: I was reminded of a bible verse (paraphrased): Do not call unholy what I have deemed holy

That moment changed something in me. I still struggle sometimes. But now I understand that nothing is imperfect; perfection is found in imperfection.

"Grace means that all of your mistakes now serve a purpose instead of serving shame."

— Brené Brown

127

The Voice That Stayed

This happened in 1990. My mother had gone into surgery for cancer at the University of Michigan hospital—but she never made it out. The grief was overwhelming. I had just turned 30 and couldn't imagine my life without her.

After her death, I began to hear a voice in my head—gentle, loving, persistent.

"I'm all right. I'm with you. I love you."

It repeated like a mantra. I didn't dare tell anyone. I believed it was my mother, but I questioned myself constantly. Was it real, or was it just wishful thinking?

One night, unable to sleep, I silently spoke back:

"Mom, I teach this stuff. I believe this stuff. But I just don't know if this is really you."

Compelled by something I couldn't explain, I got out of bed—still in the room my sisters had shared growing up—and walked into the next room, my brother Gary's. At 2 a.m., one book on the shelf drew me in. It was titled *Death and Dying*, written by a group of Catholic priests and nuns—not the well-known one by Elisabeth Kübler-Ross. The copyright date was 1982.

I took it back with me, lay on the bed, and opened it randomly.

What I read stopped me cold.

The paragraph began with the name "Katherine"—my mother's name. It described a woman dying of cancer at the age of 68—my mother's exact age and cause of death. Then came this line, as if answering the question I had asked just minutes earlier:

"The pain became so great, I asked God to take it away."

I couldn't sleep after that. I was stunned, flooded with emotion. Hours later, I went downstairs, where my father sat quietly in the dining room. I paced nervously before finally saying, "Dad, I need to talk to you."

I told him everything—the voice, the book, the message I had just read.

He collapsed out of his chair and wept like a child. The experience overwhelmed him, too.

That was thirty-five years ago. And still, the memory holds its power.

A few nights later, I created a little ceremony with holy water and a candle beside a statue of the Virgin Mary. I prayed, "Mom, I need to ask you to leave." But the voice continued—for months, maybe years. Eventually, it softened, then faded.

I remember the day it stopped. I was working as a massage therapist in Flint when I felt it lift—like something had finally settled. I walked out of my office and told Denise, the woman I rented space from, "I think it's over. I think she's really gone."

She looked at me strangely, and maybe I should've kept that moment to myself. But I knew.

I still think of my mom often. I look at her pictures. I love her. I miss her. But I believe she stayed close until I was strong enough to let her go.

> *"Love knows not its own depth until the hour of separation."*
>
> — *Kahlil Gibran*

128

Being The Change

When I was a young girl, I had many spiritual gifts that I didn't quite understand, yet in hindsight, I see how I was perfectly positioned to share many blessings wherever I went. Particularly, I was extremely empathic, could feel the thoughts of others, and had intense compassion for all living things. Oftentimes, I found myself standing up for other kids who would get bullied, getting into all sorts of trouble myself because of it.

My parents worked a lot, so my brother and I were always sent to a local park/ summer camp where we would spend time with the local kids. One kid in particular, Jose, was a special soul with many disabilities. He was taller than most of the grown-ups there, but seemed to have the mind of a toddler, and my heart would break each morning when I would see the other children rejecting him and refusing to play.

He would sit on the bench that looked towards the sandpit, hopelessly, watching the children playing on the monkey bars and swinging each other, feeling quite alone, like he didn't belong. So one day, I sat beside him on that bench and started calling him my friend. It was very challenging to even know what to say, considering the communication barriers we had, but I think more than anything, I could feel the joy and appreciation from his soul through our eyes connecting.

I asked him if he would push me on the swing, and grabbed his hand and ran towards the playground, when the children began laughing and mocking us. I turned around and loudly said, "Well, you don't know what you're missing! Jose is so much fun and he's my best friend!". Although for a moment, he looked sad that the other children were being so mean, he soon forgot, and the playground was filled with our loud giggles and laughter as he pushed me higher and higher on the swing. We spent the entire week together, sharing our lunch, sitting under the tree, and playing catch. I felt so blessed to have shared that with him!

The weekend passed, and on a Monday, I was so excited to go back to the park to see my new friend, only to realize that he wasn't there. The entire week went by, and no sign of Jose anywhere. I asked one of the counselors where he might be, and they said they didn't know. The following week, as my father dropped us off in the morning at the park, I saw from a distance all the counselors gathered together and a lady wearing black speaking to them. I could feel everyone's sadness and grief, but I couldn't quite understand what was happening. I said good morning, and one of the leaders asked if I would come and sit down with them. The lady who was with them happened to be Jose's mother. They sat me down and she introduced herself, and she began thanking me for the beautiful friendship and kindness and love that I had shown Jose. She knew how challenging it was with the other kids, but she had never seen him so happy.

To my shock and disbelief, my dear friend Jose had passed away peacefully in his sleep. I did not know in any way what his fate was, and for the first time in my life, I experienced grief and loss as a young child. I did what any little girl would do: I cried and cried and wanted to go home.

Many years later, in hindsight, I am always reminded how we are perfectly planted wherever our Love is needed. For our beloved Creator only asks for a willing heart and takes care of everything else.

As Jesus has shared in his teachings, a willing heart is not simply an attitude, but a reflection of a transformed life, characterized by love, faith, and a desire to serve God and others. It's about aligning one's desire with God's Will, and responding to His call with joy and generosity. As children, it is in our state of innocence that we capture this essence so beautifully. May we always remember to be bold in following the whispers of God.

"Let nothing be done through selfish ambition or conceit, but in lowliness of mind, let each esteem others better than themselves. Let each of you look out, not only for their own interest, but also for the interest of others."

— Philippians 2:3–4

129

The Holiest Place I've Ever Been

I was in my thirties, working in home health, still rooted in the Southern Baptist tradition. That's when I was assigned to care for a Catholic priest in the final days of his life. I didn't expect to feel such a connection, but I did. After he passed, I attended his funeral mass. It was the first time I had ever stepped inside a Catholic church.

And something shifted.

The incense, the music, the rhythm of kneeling and standing, the quiet reverence—it all felt deeply sacred. There was more scripture read aloud than I'd ever heard in a Baptist service. Everything I had been taught about Catholics turned out not to be true. I began attending daily mass. My husband, at the time, was not happy about it. I told him more than once that, as the head of our household, he could ask me to stop—and being the submissive wife, I would.

The time I spent between patients, driving from one home to another, became a sacred space. I used those moments to pray.

Eventually, the tension at home grew, and I offered up a prayer. I told God, "Even though I feel pulled, my husband wants me to stop going to daily mass, so I will. But if You want me there, You'll have to put me there."

Not even an hour later, I got a call from the office. They had a new patient for me: a cloistered Carmelite nun—living inside a monastery.

That afternoon, I found myself behind the monastery walls—walls no one enters without special permission from the bishop. But because I was a nurse, I was allowed in.

After the visit, I stepped quietly into the public side of the chapel. As I sat in the silence, I felt it—a presence so gentle, so profound, it can only be described as holy. It was as if I had walked into a room where love and peace lived.

I knew I was standing on sacred ground.

"Holy ground is not a place. It's a moment when your soul recognizes God was there all along."

— Author unknown

130

The Light That Let Me Let Go

My daughter Jeanne had been ill for ten years. Once again, she was back in the hospital so they could run tests and try to understand what was happening. I came to visit, and we spoke about a bone marrow biopsy they planned for the next day. Both of us felt she was too weak to go through with it. I didn't stay long after that.

As I was leaving, I pulled into the parking garage behind a van. The license plate caught my eye. It read simply: "SOON."

A chill ran through me.

I drove home, heart heavy. When I pulled into the driveway, the garage door was open—and I saw the image of Jeanne's deceased father standing there. He didn't say a word, but I knew. It was a loving warning. Our precious daughter was going to pass.

The next morning, I got up early, ready to be with Jeanne through the biopsy. But as I drove, there was a major accident on the highway. I realized I was going to be too late. I rushed into the hospital, anxious to reach her room.

A nurse saw me coming. "Ann..." she began, and I braced myself. "Your daughter passed this morning."

I broke down, sobbing. The staff found a quiet place where I could wait for my family to arrive. As I sat alone, grief consumed me—especially the thought that Jeanne had passed without a family member there to hold her hand.

When my family arrived, we went together into her room. The very first thing I saw stopped me. A warm, loving light surrounded her face and upper body. Her face looked peaceful—radiant, even.

In that moment, I knew she was showing me that she had made it. She was in heaven. And she was okay. We prayed over her, and I kissed her cheek goodbye. As we left her room, the sorrow that I hadn't been there was replaced by a deep peace. She hadn't been alone.

And somehow, neither was I.

"Even in her passing, she was wrapped in light, and I knew heaven had come to meet her."

— Author unknown

With Deepest Gratitude

What a journey we've been on! It has meant so much to us that you have taken the time to share a piece of your heart. It is God's will that we share instead of project onto the world, and we are blessed that you have chosen to be a vessel of light that is needed more than ever.

We've read your stories with our hearts open, felt your pain, experienced your joy as we know what you go through, for we are all holy children of God and are in this together. Some of you asked to be anonymous or to use only first names, and we have honored that to the best of our ability.

We had no idea how this was going to unfold, and as it did, we were amazed at the depth of stories from all walks of life. The undercurrent in each story revealed that God is truly at work in each of our lives. There is no doubt, and your stories have shown us that time and time again.

Our prayer is that each person who reads your inspiring stories feels the presence of the Holy Spirit that is within all of us—the Christ light. There is nothing on this Earth that can match the love that lies in our hearts and souls. We pray that you are blessed by each page, for our intention is to come from love and to speak to the hearts that cry out for that.

With love and gratitude,

Joy LeChien and Linda Perry

To All Who Shared Their Hearts With Us

Ahley Jacobs

Janet Sellers Ellis

Arcely Mitchum

Braydon Miller

Chedem Djahit

Cheryl Fraizer

Dakota

David Rosenthal

Diane Fries

Euna Houston

Garland Landrith

George Norwood

Hazel Hughins

JCody Smith

James Campbell

James Snyder

Jean Maynard

JoAnn Jordon

John Benevides

Judith Finneren

Judy Wickson

KarYn Lee

Lena Nowmos

Linda Wright Schultz

Lisa Meyer Martin

Lorena Morales

Alan Marsh

Anonymous

Bonnie Bishop Case

Carol Clausson

Cheryl Crumpler Harris

Chris Salbego

Danny Wright

Debbie Blevins

Elaine Abbott

Gale Cochran-Smith

Gary Johnson

Hannah Cohen

Iveta Makarewich

Jack Jamison

James Osbourn

Javonna Strafuss

Jennifer Gibson

John Austin

John Dumas

Judy Butler

Julian Mann

Karo Miller

Linda Mae Costello

Lisa

Lollie Bratcher

Mark Campbell

Marybeth Noriega

Mildred Crump

Monique Thebeau

Nicol Tillou

Pauline Bradbury

Rhonda & Jerome Hagood

Sandra Jackson

Sarah Gregory

Sharmila Vadi

Sherry Grady

Susan Molnar

Tom Durrant

Vicki Hoover

Taleen Khatchadourian

Ranae Waldrip

Maya Wang

Monica Brillhart

Nancy Cox

Nicole Mira Simon

Rachel Dolan

Roger Blakiston

Sandy Sue Henkel

Sarah McClasson

Sharon Wagner

Sue Emison

Tiffany Markson

Tomas Ybanez

Dean Soupal

Ann LeChien Smerek

Michele Buckley

About the Authors

Following the success of their first book, *Poetry from the Heart: Searching for God in Everyday Life*, and the creation of their inspirational card deck *Messages from the Mother*, Joy LeChien and Linda Perry have continued their collaboration—gathering voices and stories from around the world that reveal the presence of the sacred in everyday life.

Joy LeChien has a deep calling to serve those who are often overlooked—the elderly, children, and individuals navigating mental health challenges. Her background as a special education teacher and mental health case worker has shaped her compassionate approach to the world. Today, she offers transportation and a safe, listening presence to those on their way to medical appointments. Joy is also a novelist and writer whose work reflects a tender reverence for humanity. Her novel, *Pieces of Us*, explores the healing power of connection and love.

Linda Perry is a watercolor artist with a spiritual lens, a Certified Zentangle Teacher (CZT), and a former home health nurse whose life was profoundly reshaped by a life-threatening illness and vision loss. Rather than retreat, Linda turned more fully toward creativity and the Divine. Her paintings and words reflect joy, intuition, and a deep spiritual connection. Linda's original artwork graces the cover of this book, as well as their earlier works. She shares her reflections and creative journey at www.TheArtofLindaPerry.com, where spirit and creativity meet.

Quotes and Verses

At the end of each story in this collection, you'll find a quote or scripture verse that reflects the theme or spirit of that story—a final note of insight, comfort, or blessing.

1. "You may not always see the result, but no act of love is ever lost."

— St. Teresa of Calcutta

.2. "Grace is not part of consciousness; it is the amount of light in our souls, not knowledge nor reason."

— Pope Francis

3. "Be still and know that I am God."

— Psalm 46:10

4. "I once was lost, but now am found; was blind, but now I see." — John Newton

5. "Let justice roll on like a river, righteousness like a never-failing stream." — Amos 5:24

6. "You cannot know the outcome which is best. And so you trust it all to One who does."

— A Course in Miracles

7. "There are angels who walk this earth, disguised as daughters-in-law."

— Author unknown

8. "The earth is the Lord's, and everything in it, the world, and all who live in it." — Psalm 24:1

9. "Indeed, the very hairs of your head are all numbered. Don't be afraid; you are worth more than many sparrows."

— Luke 12:7

10. "He said to her, 'Daughter, your faith has healed you. Go in peace and be freed from your suffering.'" — Mark 5:34

11. "There is no death because the Son of God is like his Father. Nothing you can do can change Eternal Love."

— A Course in Miracles

12. "The soul always knows what to do to heal itself. The challenge is to silence the mind."

— Caroline Myss

13. "We shall never know all the good that a simple smile can do." — Mother Teresa

14. "Trust in the Lord with all your heart and lean not on your own understanding; in all your ways submit to him, and he will make your paths straight."

— Proverbs 3:5–6

15. "Love is the bridge between you and everything."

---Rumi

16. "Sometimes a seemingly random moment is the answer to a prayer you didn't know you were praying."

— Unknown

17. "If you ever feel overwhelmed, remember that even roses grow in thorns."

— Unknown

18. "Every loving thought is true. Everything else is a cry for healing and help, regardless of the form it takes."

— A Course in Miracles

19. "Perhaps this is the moment for which you have been created."

— Esther 4:14

20. "Even in the brokenness, there is blessing."

— Morgan Harper Nichols

21. "Be strong and courageous. Do not be afraid; do not be discouraged, for the Lord your God will be with you wherever you go."

— Joshua 1:9

22. "Faith is taking the first step even when you don't see the whole staircase."

— Martin Luther King Jr.

23. "I am sustained by the Love of God."

— A Course in Miracles

24. "Therefore encourage one another and build each other up, just as in fact you are doing."

— 1 Thessalonians 5:11

25. "The steps of a good man are ordered by the Lord: and he delighteth in his way."

— Psalm 37:23

26.

"The Lord will rescue me from every evil attack and will bring me safely to his heavenly kingdom." 2 Timothy 4:18

27. "Coincidence is God's way of remaining anonymous."

— Albert Einstein

28. "He will cover you with his feathers, and under his wings you will find refuge; his faithfulness will be your shield and rampart."

— Psalm 91:4

29. "You will keep in perfect peace those whose minds are steadfast, because they trust in you."

— Isaiah 26:3

30. "Blessed are the peacemakers, for they will be called children of God."

— Matthew 5:9

31 "Many are the plans in a person's heart, but it is the Lord's purpose that prevails."

— Proverbs 19:21

32. "God goes with me wherever I go."

— A Course in Miracles

33. "For I know the plans I have for you," declares the Lord, "plans to prosper you and not to harm you, plans to give you hope and a future."

— Jeremiah 29:11

34. "He makes me lie down in green pastures, he leads me beside quiet waters, he restores my soul."

— Psalm 23:2–3

35 "Be kind and compassionate to one another, forgiving each other, just as in Christ God forgave you."

— Ephesians 4:32

36. "My grace is sufficient for you, for my power is made perfect in weakness."

— 2 Corinthians 12:9

37. "The best way to find yourself is to lose yourself in the service of others."

— Mahatma Gandhi

38. "Wherever there is a human being, there is an opportunity for kindness."

— Seneca

39. "Underneath are the everlasting arms." — Deuteronomy 33:27

40 "Love is the way I walk in gratitude."

— A Course in Miracles, Lesson 195

"Let all that you do be done in love."

— 1 Corinthians 16:14

41. "I am with you and will watch over you wherever you go."

— Genesis 28:15

42 "There is no order of difficulty in miracles. One is not 'harder' or 'bigger' than another."

— A Course in Miracles,

43. "Do not forget to show hospitality to strangers, for by so doing some have entertained angels without knowing it."

— Hebrews 13:2

44. "To forgive is to set a prisoner free and discover that the prisoner was you."

— Lewis B. Smedes

45 "Grief is in two parts. The first is loss. The second is the remaking of life."

— Anne Roiphe

46 "In a spiritual encounter, all relationships are seen as mirrors of the self, while the heart remains open to freely express and receive love without possessiveness."

— Michael Mirdad

47. "Before they call, I will answer; while they are still speaking, I will hear."

— Isaiah 65:24

48. Love your enemies, do good to those who hate you."

— Luke 6:27

49. You didn't come here to find God. You came here to remember you never left."

— Michael Mirdad

50 "He will give his angels charge over you, to guard you in all your ways."

— Psalm 91:11

51. "In their hearts humans plan their course, but the Lord establishes their steps."

— Proverbs 16:9

52 "You will seek me and find me when you seek me with all your heart."

— Jeremiah 29:13

53. "Death is not extinguishing the light; it is only putting out the lamp because the dawn has come."

— Rabindranath Tagore

54. "I am not what happened to me. I am what I choose to become."

— Carl Jung

55 "When we lose one blessing, another is often most unexpectedly given in its place."

— C.S. Lewis

56 "To one who has faith, no explanation is necessary. To one without faith, no explanation is possible." —Thomas Aquinas

57 "God writes the Gospel not in the Bible alone, but also on trees, and in the flowers and clouds and stars."

— Martin Luther

58 "The Lord will watch over your coming and going both now and forevermore."

— Psalm 121:8

59. "Your father knows what you need before you ask him."

— Matthew 6:8

60 "Out of difficulties grow miracles."

— Jean de La Bruyère

61 "The prayer of a righteous person is powerful and effective."

— James 5:16

62 "Forgiveness is the key to peace and freedom."

— A Course in Miracles

63 "Peace I leave with you; my peace I give you. I do not give to you as the world gives. Do not let your hearts be troubled, and do not be afraid."

— John 14:27

64 "What we have once enjoyed, we can never lose. All that we love deeply becomes a part of us."

— Helen Keller

65 "There is no death. Death is but a change of mind."

— A Course in Miracles,

66 "Every day is a second chance."

— Unknown

67. "What the caterpillar calls the end of the world, the master calls a butterfly."

— Richard Bach

68 "And we know that in all things God works for the good of those who love him, who have been called according to his purpose."

— Romans 8:28

69. "Ask, and it will be given to you; seek, and you will find; knock, and the door will be opened to you."

— Matthew 7:7

70. "You turned my mourning into dancing; you removed my sackcloth and clothed me with joy."

— Psalm 30:11

71. "If you knew who walks beside you on the way that you have chosen, fear would be impossible."

— A Course in Miracles

72. "Nothing... will be able to separate us from the love of God that is in Christ Jesus our Lord." — Romans 8:38–39

73 "God is within her, she will not fall; God will help her at break of day."

— Psalm 46:5

74 "Mary is more Mother than Queen." — St. Thérèse of Lisieux

75. "And now these three remain: faith, hope and love. But the greatest of these is love." — 1 Corinthians 13:13 (NIV)

76 "...and a little child shall lead them."

— Isaiah 11:6

77 "And after the fire came a gentle whisper."

— 1 Kings 19:12

78. But the Comforter, which is the Holy Ghost, whom the Father will send in my name, shall teach you all things, and bring all things to your remembrance, whatsoever I have said unto you. Peace I leave with you, my peace I give unto you: not as the world giveth, give I unto you. Let not your heart be troubled, neither let it be afraid.

--1 John 14: 26-27

79. And call on me in the day of trouble; I will deliver you, and you will honor me.

Psalm 50:15

80. "The Lord will keep you from all harm—He will watch over your life."

— Psalm 121:7

81 "He will wipe every tear from their eyes. There will be no more death or mourning or crying or pain, for the old order of things has passed away."

— Revelation 21:4

82 "The light shines in the darkness, and the darkness has not overcome it."

---John 1-5

83 May the God of hope fill you with all joy and peace in believing, so that by the power of the holy spirit you may abound in hope.

--- Romans 15:13

84 "The Lord is good to all; he has compassion on all he has made."

— Psalm 145:9

85 "Even in the darkest moments, love gives hope."

St. John Paul II (2001 address after 9/11)

86 "Where there is injury, let me sow pardon; where there is doubt, faith; where there is despair, hope; where there is darkness, light."

--St Francis of Assisi

87 "Abide in me, and I in you."

— John 15:4

88. "The angel of the Lord encamps around those who fear him, and he delivers them."

— Psalm 34:7

89 "We have different gifts, according to the grace given to each of us. If your gift is prophesying, then prophesy in accordance with your faith."

--Romans 12:6

90 "Rock bottom became the solid foundation on which I rebuilt my life."

—J.K. Rowling

91. "When the soul is ready, the path appears."

— Author

92 "Truly I tell you, whatever you did for one of the least of these brothers and sisters of mine, you did for me."

--Matthew 25:40

93 "He has shown you, O mortal, what is good. And what does the Lord require of you? To act justly and to love mercy and to walk humbly with your God."

— Micah 6:8 (NIV)

94 "Therefore, as God's chosen people, holy and dearly loved, clothe yourselves with compassion, kindness, humility, gentleness and patience."

--Colossians 3:12

95. "What you are seeking is also seeking you."

— Rumi

96. "You may never know what results come of your actions. But if you do nothing, there will be no result."

--Mahtma Gandhi

97. "There is no such thing as chance or coincidence. Every moment of your life is guided by a greater wisdom." — White Eagle

98. "If only you could see how close God is to you always—not far off in the heavens, but quietly shining in the smallest moments of your life."

— White Eagle

99. "When you pass through the waters, I will be with you; and when you pass through the rivers, they will not sweep over you." --Isaiah 43:2

100. "Don't you know yet?

It is your Light that lights the worlds."

— Rumi

101 "Nothing real can be threatened. Nothing unreal exists. Herein lies the peace of God."

— A Course in Miracles

102 "He heals the brokenhearted and binds up their wounds."

— Psalm 147:3

103 "To give and to receive are one in truth."

— A Course in Miracles,

104 "You are altogether beautiful, my darling; there is no flaw in you."

— Song of Songs 4:7

105 "In the last days, God says, I will pour out my Spirit on all people.

Your sons and daughters will prophesy,

your young men will see visions,

your old men will dream dreams."

—Acts 2:17

106 "The whole universe is conspiring to help you"

— Paulo Coelho

107 "For He satisfies the thirsty and fills the hungry with good things."

Psalm 107:9

108 "Until one has loved an animal, a part of one's soul remains unawakened."

— Anatole France

109 "Christ has no body now but yours, no hands, no feet on earth but yours..."

St. Teresa of Avila

110 "Give, and it will be given to you. A good measure, pressed down, shaken together and running over, will be poured into your lap."

Luke 6:38

111 "Blessed are those who mourn, for they shall be comforted."

— Matthew 5:4

112 "Whoever saves a life, it is considered as if he saved an entire world."

--- from the Talmud, Tractate Sanhedrin 4:9

113 "Love and compassion are necessities, not luxuries. Without them, humanity cannot survive."

— Dalai Lama

114 "You make known to me the path of life; you will fill me with joy in your presence, with eternal pleasures at your right hand."

— Psalm 16:11

"I praise you because I am fearfully and wonderfully made; your works are wonderful, I know that full well."

— Psalm 139:14

115 "Love is the only force capable of transforming an enemy into a friend."

--Dr. Martin Luther King, Jr

116."" Jesus said, 'Let the little children come to me, and do not hinder them, for the kingdom of heaven belongs to such as these.'"

— Matthew 19:14

117. "Even to your old age and gray hairs, I am he, I am he who will sustain you. I have made you and I will carry you; I will sustain you and I will rescue you." Isaiah 46:4

118 "Love bears all things, believes all things, hopes all things, endures all things Love never fails." — 1 Corinthians 13:7–8

119. "You are not a drop in the ocean. You are the entire ocean in a drop."

—Rumi

120. "Faith does not make things easy; it makes them possible." — Luke 1:37

121. "Veterinarians may treat animals, but they also heal the hearts of those who love them."

— Unknown

122. "Teach us to number our days, that we may gain a heart of wisdom."

— Psalm 90:12

123. "You do not need to seek love, only to remove the barriers you have built against it." — A Course in Miracles

124. "You were never searching alone. The One you seek has always walked beside you."

— Author unknown

125. "I will restore you to health and heal your wounds," declares the Lord.

— Jeremiah 30:17

126. "Grace means that all of your mistakes now serve a purpose instead of serving shame."

— *Brené Brown*

127. "Love knows not its own depth until the hour of separation."

— Kahlil Gibran

128. "Let nothing be done through selfish ambition or conceit, but in lowliness of mind, let each esteem others better than themselves. Let each of you look out, not only for their own interest, but also for the interest of others."--Philippians 2:3–4

129. "Holy ground is not a place. It's a moment when your soul recognizes God was there all along."

— Author unknown

130. "Even in her passing, she was wrapped in light, and I knew heaven had come to meet her."

—Author unknown

Your Story Matters

As you come to the end of these stories, we hope they've stirred memories of moments when someone made a difference in your life—or when you were that someone for another. May these reflections remind you that every act of kindness, every bit of light, matters. And may you continue to walk gently, knowing that even ordinary steps can leave sacred footprints.

If you have a story of your own that belongs on holy ground, we would be honored to read it. You're welcome to share it with us at sacredgroundstories@gmail.com.

www.ingramcontent.com/pod-product-compliance
Lightning Source LLC
Chambersburg PA
CBHW060042150626
46556CB00018BA/2264